Fired Up, Frantic, and Freaked Out

Training Crazy Dogs from Over-the-Top to Under Control

Laura VanArendonk Baugh
CPDT-KA KPACTP

Æclipse Press
Indianapolis, IN

Copyright 2013 Laura VanArendonk Baugh
Cover design by Laura VanArendonk Baugh and
    Alena Van Arendonk
Author portrait by Elemental Photography
Technical editing by Casey Lomonaco
Interior photos pages 25, 67, 77 by Alena Van Arendonk
Cover photos and interior photos pages 13, 47, 59, 91, 99,
    117, 123, 133 by Fotolia
Interior photos pages iv, 109, 147 by Laura VanArendonk
    Baugh

ISBN 978-0-9859349-2-7
Library of Congress Control Number 2012922445

www.Aeclipse-Press.com

Chaucer was the first dog I ever clicked. Without her brilliance, I might not have gone further.
1999–2003

About this book

A number of people have been asking when I was going to write a book. "I don't have to," was my usual answer. "There are so many good training books out there already."

But gradually I began to realize several things:

- 🐾 I see a lot of referrals for dogs which are basically over-aroused for one reason or another — aggression, fear, fear-aggression, joy, or just plain over-stimulated.
- 🐾 I was spending a good two-thirds or more of my training career using a very similar protocol with all these dogs, with success.
- 🐾 Many clients would have benefitted from a more-detailed follow-along guide.

As it turns out, I know a fair bit about arousal in dogs, not in little part due to my excellent instructor Laevatein, a hair-trigger Doberman bitch who had to learn stationary behaviors in mere eighths of a second. It would be good to share what she has taught me.

While I absolutely love discussing the science of behavior with other nerds, this book is intended primarily as a guideline for practical application, a sort of follow-along-at-home resource, and any sort of academic discussion only secondarily. I will use scientific terms properly, but I'll use a number of other terms for easy layman reference or explanation.

Acknowledgements

I most certainly did not come up with all this myself; the proverbial giants on whose shoulders this dwarf stands form a long line stretching back through Karen Pryor, Bob Bailey & Marian Breland Bailey, B.F. Skinner, Premack, Pavlov.... More recently we have many brilliant trainers whom I am both pleased to know and honored to call colleagues, who have brought out new research and applications. I daren't try to list them all, lest I miss one!

Many, though, you will find mentioned here. And sometimes a brilliant mind and a semi-gloss mind might discover an idea at the same time, working at similar concepts in parallel tracks. I once learned the inimitable Helix Fairweather and I were, on opposite sides of the country, both using the phrase "get out of Dodge" for very similar management techniques, though we had never discussed it. And what I do with matwork is very like what Leslie McDevitt recommends in her hugely helpful book *Control Unleashed*. No usurpation of ideas in intended!

While talking with clients I often find myself quoting Kathy Sdao, or I may use a catch-phrase popularized by Alexandra Kurland. I think it's imperative to give credit where credit is due, and I will try to cite these influences where appropriate.

And I owe an enormous thanks to Casey Lomonaco, who edited this with an eye to both science and accessibility. You're fabulous.

Chapter 1 Help, My Dog Is Crazy!

LAEV IS EAGER FOR HER TURN!

So, your dog is nuts.

Well, not *nuts*, really. Just, well, over the top. In certain situations. But he's a really good dog normally.

Or someone has said he's troubled in some way, fearful or reactive or hyper or generally not always coping with his environment. Is this program for you?

What Is an Agitated Dog, Anyway?

Good question!

An agitated dog is any dog so caught up in his emotions or innate responses that he cannot think rationally, respond to cues, or control his reactions. There are many examples regularly seen on our sidewalks, homes, parks, and dog sport venues:

🐾 A dog barks excitedly at the front door, so eager to greet his visiting friends that he doesn't respond to his owner trying to get him to sit or move back from the door.

- A dog barks worriedly at the front door, ignoring his owner's reassurances. He doesn't quiet or relax, moving alternately toward and away from the door in conflict.
- A dog is so stimulated by his favorite sport — agility, protection, lure coursing, etc. — that he misses important cues or can't control himself, resulting in broken start line stays, poor or incorrect responses, etc.

On the surface, these look like very different issues — the dog is distracted, the dog is afraid, the dog is excited. But fundamentally, the dog is in a limbic, reactive state of mind instead of being in a cognitive, proactive state of mind, and that means he can't — sometimes physically can't — respond to known cues.

Changing Behavior to Change Emotion

So it appears we have to change the dog's emotions, yes? There are a number of training protocols out there to do just that, based on **desensitization** and **classical counter-conditioning**. But while these do work, they typically take much longer than we are often willing or able to grant.

Dr. Jesús Rosales-Ruiz, Associate Professor in the Department of Behavior Analysis at the University of North Texas, points out beautifully that we aren't required to take this approach. "Psychologists change emotions to change behavior, which is great for the pharmaceutical industry. Behaviorists change the behavior to change the emotions."[1]

One human example he offers is that of a child who hates or fears math[2]. That child will only change her opinion of math if she gains confidence in the skills (behaviors) necessary to succeed at it; no pep talk is going to make a real or permanent change in her view.

"But He *Knows!*"

One hallmark characteristic of the agitated dog is the owner's plaintive cry, "But he *knows* what 'sit' means! He's so good at it anywhere else! It's just when he sees a delivery truck that he won't do it!"

A dog who doesn't know behaviors or cues may or may not be an agitated dog; he might just be uneducated! But the well-trained dog who just can't respond reliably in a trigger situation may need help to get mentally unwound from about the axle.

This makes our job as trainers twofold: Get the dog back into his own skull, so that he can think, and make sure he knows the cues we're giving.

What Do You Mean By That?

A lot of people ask, quite reasonably, what I mean by "the dog can't make himself respond." If he knows the

---

[1] Rosales-Ruiz, Jesús. Curso Internacional de Adiestradores Caninos. Mexico City. 23 July 2011.

[2] Just as in dogs, aggression is usually rooted in discomfort or fear!

behavior, and if the cue is under **stimulus control** (reliably trained), why on earth wouldn't the dog behave as he's been taught? Even if he's excited or overwrought, he still *knows* what we're asking, right?

Well, yes, but it isn't really accessible at the moment.

Imagine for a moment that you and your friend are returning to your car after a movie one night. The parking lot is dark and you have your keys in your hand — but as two men in dark jackets separate and move to flank you, you realize your keys won't be a bit of help. One man has a knife in his hand, the other points a gun. You're seventy feet from the theater door and no one else is near you. Your heart is racing, your breath is catching, your mind is whirling.

And then your friend asks, "Hey, what's seven times eight?"

Under normal circumstances, you'd be able to answer that question in a reasonable time. But in this situation, you're likely to ignore the friend completely (if you even hear the question), or perhaps even snap that it's a stupid request at such a dire moment! If your friend insists, for reasons utterly beyond your comprehension, that you answer, you will need extra time to work out the solution, or you might get the math wrong. You probably can't respond immediately with the correct answer.

This doesn't happen just in distress, either. Instead of a

dangerous situation, imagine now that you're about to welcome home a beloved family member who has just returned from extended military deployment or a lengthy hospital stay. As he's walking in the door, your aunt asks you a basic math problem. Are you any more likely to respond promptly and correctly now?

That's what is happening inside the agitated dog. Emotion and stress (whether good or bad) have taken over and are inhibiting some cognitive functions of the brain.

Even if the behavior is normally fluent, when the brain is limbic and reactive, you might not be able to respond normally.

That can be a good thing — in the mugging scenario, for example, it's foolish to waste brain cells on math instead of escape or defense plans! But the agitated dog has no concept of place or degrees. While the wild and overjoyed greeting of a family member after a long or dangerous absence might be acceptable, it's utterly inappropriate to introduce yourself to a new neighbor in the same way.

So How Do We Fix It?

In short, we're going to teach the dog how to interrupt and manage his own arousal.

For some dogs, we're going to teach them that they

actually have a choice in how they react to triggers; many have had only one option on their menu for so long that they don't realize it's even possible to meet someone at the door calmly, for example.

Why This Won't Work

Quite often, by the time I meet an agitated dog, his owners are already frustrated and exhausted. They may have worked with other trainers, read books or magazines, or watched television, and from these they might have alternate ideas on training techniques. Consequently, I've heard a variety of reasons why training won't work, in general or for this particular dog. Let's cover the most popular.

"He's not interested in food while he's reacting."

Of course he's not; he's busy reacting.

When working with fear or aggression, I require clients to use food as a reinforcer. There are several reasons for this, which we'll cover later, but the statement is often met with, "We tried that, but he's not interested in treats."

Well, that only makes sense, if you think about it; in the mugging scenario above, would you be interested if your friend offered you a candy bar at that moment, or would you think her insanely detached from reality?

What we will do will rely upon gradual approximations

and controlled exposure to raise the dog's thresholds and skills in preparation to meet — and cope with — triggers. As we'll see, one reason I require food is to make sure the triggers aren't outrunning the new skills. If the dog doesn't eat, we're doing it wrong.

"He's just too excited; this can't work."

This usually comes from the owner who has reached out for help, but just doesn't have much faith anymore that anything can be done. Often this owner feels like she's already tried most other options, with little to no improvement. In some cases, previous well-intended but misguided training may have even exacerbated the very problems she was trying to solve.

Generally, though, this protest is rooted more in emotion than fact. Your dog is special and unique, but he's not so special and unique that science doesn't apply to him!

Now it is true that some dogs need more than behavioral intervention; when I meet client dogs who exhibit symptoms of severe or generalized anxiety, or another medical condition, I refer them to a veterinarian also well-versed in behavior and they often return with a prescription[3]. As I explain to the owners, drugs do not change behavior — generally, you shouldn't see a significant difference if the dog is on the proper drug and dosage — but drugs do allow the brain to absorb and

---

[3] See more on medications and training in Chapter 12.

process the information provided in training. Medication and training must work together, as will be discussed later.

> "That's just who he is, and it's wrong and cruel to want to change it."

Some people do feel strongly about asserting their will on another entity, and I respect that. But training does not have to be — should not ever be — cruel or disrespectful.

First, our training will be all about rewarding good behavior, without punishment. Sometimes people are reluctant to train simply because they don't realize they can do it while maintaining a happy, friendly relationship with their dogs.

> *"That's an interesting combination of stuff," said the cashier at the home improvement store. "What are you making?"*
>
> *"I teach dog training classes, and these will be props for the dogs to work with."*
>
> *"Oh, that sounds fun! Oh, no, probably not. You'd have to yell at the dogs a lot."*
>
> *"Not at all! We don't yell, ever."*
>
> *"Really? You can train like that?"*
>
> *"Really. You should come and see."*
>
> *And she did, and she enrolled her dog in class.*

Other times, people assume that the dog's "natural" state

is also the dog's preferred state. This isn't always the case!

A dog who is anxious, afraid, or fearful to the point of aggression is *not* happier that way. I work with dogs who are nervous in their own homes — who wants to live that way? Far from it being wrong or cruel to try and change that, I think it is inhumane *not* to try to improve their mental health and quality of life.

Even a hyper dog might not be enjoying himself as much as it appears. Frantic behavior often looks happy, with jumping and tail-wagging and licking, but in fact the dog may be just as stressed as the dog hiding under the table, only expressing it differently. While he may not be afraid, he is not in control of his own emotions and reactions, and that can be unpleasant.

If we bring dogs into our human society, it is then our responsibility to teach them how to be comfortable and happy in it, and how to behave as welcome members so they can participate in it.

An untrained dog might seem more "natural," but his life isn't really any happier than his trained cousin's. The untrained dog must be put away when guests come to visit, because he jumps on them or barks annoyingly. The untrained dog isn't welcome in the room while the family eats, because he's pushy and rude at the table. The untrained dog goes on fewer walks, because he's less fun to walk, and rarely gets to travel to new and interesting places with his family. Meanwhile, the trained dog is rarely separated from his human friends and is welcome nearly everywhere he goes.

Training, far from being cruel, is one of the greatest gifts we can give our pets.

> "He's not stressed, distressed, afraid, or frantic, he's just stubborn."

A thorough rebuttal would require more explanation of a dog's emotions and motivations than this book encompasses. Generally, we can find our way past this protest with a simple test.

I am holding in my hand the most fabulous concoction of amazing treats we can invent. The dog can have them all, if he can just bring himself to stop barking at the door and sit for two seconds. Can he do it? Or do we really think he's deliberately spiting himself out of liver, steak, and cheese, just so he can enjoy raging at the door with an elevated heart rate and bloodshot eyes?

No, I didn't think so, either. (And it works for less extreme cases as well!)

> "I don't have time to train the dog."

I can't help you.

Actually, I can — the training sessions in this program are very short, often just 30 seconds long. Anyone can fit that into his day, even while reheating leftovers in the microwave. I'm a huge fan of what I call microwave training.

But if this protest is used as a cover for "I'm not really interested in training the dog," then I honestly can't help. As a trainer, I can tell you what's possible and give you tools to accomplish it, but I can't motivate you to do anything about it.

If you're actually worried about time, however, take heart — training sessions will be short and flexible, so you can work them into your schedule as convenient. You may find that your rate of progress far exceeds your expectations.

Let's Get Started

So, enough talk — let's train!

Or, let's get prepared to train.

Chapter 2 Where Do We Start?

THIS DOG WOULD REALLY APPRECIATE SOME HELP.

It's best to start in an area with few distractions, where the dog can focus wholly on learning. All dogs have *somewhere* they can be relaxed and themselves — or they should, anyway; abused dogs may not, and dogs with an anxiety disorder may not. These special cases require special treatment.

But for those dogs who become agitated in a trigger situation, we're going to start well away from that situation. Learning happens in a mind which is still engaged, and so we need to begin teaching the dog new behaviors and skills while he is still under threshold.

Teach the Skills First

Skills have to be learned before they can be used. That seems fairly self-evident, and yet I often see someone struggling to physically control an over-excited dog while trying to instruct or manhandle it into a more tractable frame of mind. This is inefficient, at best.

I had a client recently who did not want to waste time on foundations, who wanted to have the first lesson in the trigger situation. After all, the dog was already well-behaved at home! I explained that this was equivalent to taking a new student driver onto the interstate and only then trying to explain gear shifts, turn signals, and left and right pedals. You need to have the skills under stress — therefore you have to learn them before you're under stress.

Get Organized

So, put the dog aside for a moment, and let's get ourselves organized for smart, efficient training....

Identify a Safe, Relaxing Location

How safe and how relaxing? Ideally you'll be training off-leash. If you're uncomfortable with that idea, worried that your dog might be distracted or triggered, you're probably not in the right place!

For most people, the living room or kitchen is an ideal starting location. If you have other pets, put them away[4]; your learner doesn't need the distraction of anyone muscling in for treats or attention. Likewise, minimize human interference. Distractions come *later* in the learning process.

---

[4] It's a good idea to occasionally separate pets, anyway, to prevent co-dependence or distress when alone. Stuff a Kong™ or provide another puzzle toy to occupy separated pets and teach them that time alone is fun!

Assemble Your Materials

Most of what we will need is very easy to come by and very inexpensive.

A mat

I almost always use mat-work in this protocol; it makes it easy for humans to see what's going on in the dog's head. A mat can be nearly anything: a hand towel, a placemat from the dollar store, a door mat. I recommend something portable and washable.

The mat will become your dog's security blanket and yoga mat.

I tell clients the mat will become the dog's combination security blanket and yoga mat. It can reassure an anxious dog while calming an excited one. It's important to note that the *behavior* of lying on a mat isn't the goal, but the emotional and cognitive state the dog is in while doing so.

Is the mat a crutch? Heck, yeah, it is! But crutches can be valuable tools when needed, and they can be discarded when they're no longer necessary.

"But I won't always have the mat when we're out!" Well, that may be true (though quite a few of my clients started carrying a very-portable mat on walks, vet visits, etc. once they realized its utility). But again, the mat isn't the destination, it's a point en route to the destination. It's a crutch during the healing process; use it until you don't need it.

A clicker

I *highly* recommend the use of a clicker or other discrete[5], distinct marker. This isn't because I'm addicted to the bit of plastic, it's because the process actually runs more quickly with a marker.

First, there's the issue of acquisition. Because a clicker (or other discrete conditioned reinforcer, such as a mechanical whistle, a well-executed tongue click, a penlight for deaf dogs, etc.) is non-verbal and consistent, the dog's brain doesn't waste time or get confused evaluating para-linguistic baggage ("was that *good!* a louder or more excited *good!* than this *good!* feedback? When she said I was a good dog, was that the same *good*? What about when she said *good!* while talking on the phone?").

This is going to be very simple for the dog — he's got it right, or he needs to try again. We simply don't need an analog system to convey a binary result. Because it's more efficient communication, research indicates dogs learn much faster with a neutral, discrete marker than with a human voice[6], and we have enough to train that

---

[5] This isn't "discreet" meaning "unobtrusive," but rather "discrete" meaning "individual, separate, distinct." Either I clicked or I didn't; there's no confusion or grey area.

[6] Wood, Lindsay. (2008) *Clicker Bridging Stimulus Efficacy*. Master's

we should make things as easy as possible.

Second, as long as we're mucking about in the brain, let's do it with intention and efficiency. Fear and anxiety reactions happen in the amygdala, the little backward part of the brain which reacts first and asks questions later. As it happens, the amygdala is also the part of the brain which processes marker signals. If I want to fight stress in the brain, what better way than by hijacking its home base?

We simply don't need an analog system to convey a binary result.

Food Treats

Note I am very specific here that our reinforcement will be food. Of course we can use various types of reinforcement in training, from tactile (petting) to objects and play (tug toys) and many more. But when working with arousal, and especially with fear or aggression, I almost always use food.

I joke with clients, "The dog can't pump adrenaline and saliva at the same time."

The act of eating is generally physiologically calming, as the body prepares to digest. (This might explain why we often seek comfort food

thesis, Hunter College, New York.

while under stress, too!) Thus by using food, we can combat arousal not only behaviorally, but physiologically, conditioning the body to be more relaxed. (This effect *may* be even more pronounced with soft, lick-able food, as the action induces the dog to stretch and relax jaw muscles.)

Also, how an animal takes food gives us valuable insight into what's going on in his head. An animal in immediate distress is not going to eat (remember how you wouldn't want a candy bar from your friend while you were being mugged?), but there are several stages leading toward that condition:

- 🐾 Animal takes treats readily and as gently as he has been taught
- 🐾 Animal takes treats readily, but less gently (distracted and/or losing fine motor skills)
- 🐾 Animal takes treats, but needs a second or two to orient to them (distracted, threatened, and/or losing motor skills)
- 🐾 Animal takes treats under duress (distracted, threatened)
- 🐾 Animal does not take treats (beyond threshold, animal is on the point of reacting or already is — we don't ever want to get here!)

Also, many non-food reinforcement options are themselves stimulating — playing tug, or chasing a ball, or roughhousing with a human. While all of these may be perfectly appropriate for teaching other new behaviors, they are not conducive toward conditioning the body to relax. Additionally, while calm petting can be very pleasant, it generally does not offer the very powerful reinforcement we'll want to establish to override an extreme emotional response.

I recommend very small (pea-sized or smaller) treat pieces, which should be both valuable to the dog and healthy. Often this is something which can substitute as a portion of the dog's daily diet. I may use several dozen treats in a single training session, possibly a couple hundred if we're doing advanced work or a longer session, and I don't want the dog to become either satiated or ill.[7]

Sometimes owners worry that their dogs are so excited by food they couldn't possibly relax or think while it's present, or the dog is annoyingly pushy while they have treats. Hold that thought! That is exactly the problem we're trying to address, just on a smaller scale. It'll work out, I promise.

Identify a Data-Keeping System that Works for You

I know, no one wants to keep data while they're training.

---

[7] Freeze-dried 100% meat treats (available commercially from Bravo! Raw Diet™ and other brands) generally induce tap-dancing joy in dogs while supplementing that day's dinner. If you're worried about size and quantity with small dogs, consider that I've had KPA students treat their dogs from an eyedropper during frequent, intense training. There's always a way!

You're training, for heaven's sake. You're busy. Besides, you can keep track of how you're doing in your head, right?

Unfortunately, no, you can't.

For one thing, human memory is fallible. For another, when we don't make a specific note of things, we remember unspecific notes. ("He can stay on the mat for a little while, while I'm a short distance away.") And finally, human emotion can cloud both human memory and human interpretation, potentially wasting valuable training time.

> I had a client complain that she couldn't possibly be expected to maintain the training I'd asked of her, because it was taking her a full 15 minutes to get through the door, what with having to cue the dog and treat it and whatnot, and she just didn't have that kind of time.
>
> So I pulled out ClickStats[8] and asked her to practice several repetitions of the behavior. She obliged, fussing at how long it took the dog to respond and how she couldn't do this every day. And when the app did the math, non-subjectively, it turned out they were spending an average of 16 seconds on each repetition, including treating and setting up for the next rep.

That's an extreme example, but it happens all the time.

---

[8] A clicker training app which collects data as you click to give you success ratios, reps per minute, and other data. Available for both Android and iOS.

The owner was experiencing a number of other stresses in her life, and it colored her interpretation of how her dog was working. Likewise, I've seen clients want so desperately for things to change that they push their dog too far, too quickly, which can backfire and cause serious training setbacks.

It's less nerve-wracking and safer to just keep the data.

There are many ways to keep records, and the best way is the one you can maintain!

- ClickStats or a similar record-keeping app
- Tic marks on a page in two columns, *click* and *no-click*, along with a timer.
- Counting out a specific number of treats, and then either delivering them to the dog or setting them aside to count as no-clicks afterward, subtracting from the original total to find successful reps, and a timer.
- Whatever consistently works for you!

The critical data will be your criteria, the success ratio (clicked reps/total reps) and number of clicks per minute. A sample line of records might read, "Mat in entry, two knocks outside front door, 70%," meaning the mat was in the front entry room, we were presenting two knocks on the outside of the front door, and the dog remained calm on the mat 7 reps out of 10.

You can find a simple record sheet at the end of the book or download one at www.CaninesInAction.com.

Flex Those Fingers

While operating a simple clicker and delivering a treat to the dog may appear to be easy, there is a skill to it, and it's best to practice in advance so that you can be as efficient as possible during training.

Clicking and treating is a four-beat process:

- 🐾 Click
- 🐾 Pause
- 🐾 Move the treat hand
- 🐾 Deliver

Practice this slowly, counting aloud if necessary. If you're like most, you'll find your hand wanting to move on the second beat, where there should be stillness. Solve this by placing your hand in a comfortable "station" away from your treats and concentrate on keeping it still until beat three.

Don't be surprised if your hand reverts to old habits as you train; focus on keeping your hand at its station until your mechanics are clean again. If your hand drifts, just think of it as giving you empathy for your dog and his old habits!

And Now, With the Dog

Now bring the dog into your selected location and we're ready to begin.

Or was your dog waiting there while you were gathering

a mat, a clicker, treats, and notepaper?

We're often used to letting our dogs hang in limbo while we arrange a training scenario, and it's a bad habit, especially with arousal — bad enough that it's a common cause of backsliding. Without structure or feedback, the dog will revert to habit, and right now habit is *not* what you're after.

This won't be the case forever — indeed, one of our goals will be to teach the dog to assess the situation himself and make good choices — but he's not ready for that yet. Start building good habits in yourself if you want to see them in your dog.

Chapter 3 Foundation Training

LAEV TARGETS
ENTHUSIASTICALLY ENOUGH
TO PUSH MY HAND

Now that all your materials are assembled appropriately and you've practiced your four-beat click and delivery, let's get started!

Regardless of what other behaviors may be in a dog's repertoire, I want to see him learn targeting and mat placement before we begin to do the "serious" training. These foundation behaviors will both teach him our new protocol and form the basis of his new coping skills.

Many of the over-aroused dogs I meet have no background in clicker training, and that's fine with me — a blank slate means we have no baggage to work through, allowing us to instill good habits from the beginning.

For the dog and owner who have done other types of training, this introduction to clicker training is vital. We are going to be asking for some very different approaches from both dog and handler, and both need to be comfortable with the system before we start the challenging stuff.

Even for the dog who has had extensive clicker training, I want to be sure he's in the right frame of mind. We are going to be working almost exclusively with shaping, and the dog needs to be very proactive and exploratory. I want him to approach each training session with an eagerness to figure out the riddle and guess the next step.

A dog who has been trained positively with lures or prompting is likely to struggle with this at the beginning, and a handler who is used to prompting behavior is going to feel frustrated (which will probably impede the dog's learning). It's best to get past all that before we are working in more challenging stages!

Clicker Training In A Nutshell

The purpose of this book isn't to explain the theories and techniques of clicker training, so we'll pass very quickly over this. (See the Appendix for additional resources.) But there are a few key points to keep in mind for maximum effectiveness as we work through these exercises.

Clicker training works particularly well for helping these overstimulated dogs because it encourages proactive actions instead of reactive. Rather than physically prompting, luring, or verbally coaxing a dog into an action, remain quiet and let him explore his options. We cannot train a dog to self-assess if he is never given the chance to do so.

Resist the urge to inform the dog of a mistake! Frustration does not reduce arousal, and punishment does not encourage calm self-assessment. **No-reward markers** are unnecessary. If you are training properly, your dog's error will be just as glaring to him as to you even without your moving a muscle — clicker training is all about binary feedback, and a 0 is clearly not a 1. Let him do the math.

Your mechanical skills are critical; of the three core components to good training, Timing, Criteria, and Rate of Reinforcement[9], your mechanical skills directly determine two. Practice the four-beat exercise to be sure you're giving your dog accurate information!

Splitting

We're going to talk a *lot* about splitting as we progress through training. Splitting is dividing a task or training goal into smaller, more easily accomplished pieces. It's a skill which doesn't come easily to all; we often tend to "lump" (look at bigger chunks of behavior) instead of "split" (slice a goal behavior into many smaller goals).

Splitting is essential to good training, and especially to the type of training we'll be doing. If we lump behaviors — "my dog has learned to sit in an empty room, so now

---

[9] Bob Bailey famously said that all problems a trainer might encounter will lie within the application of timing, criteria, or rate of reinforcement. And you know, I've never found an instance where that hasn't been the case....

I'll ask him to sit while the doorbell rings and guests walk in" — we're going to experience failure and frustration.

Good splitting breaks the sequence down into such easy sequential steps that the progression feels seamless. Many of these more typical steps will be suggested in the text ahead, but you may need to develop your own based on your individual needs.

Splitting can feel "slow" to those not used to it, because it's many small steps instead of fewer large ones, but in the long run training actually moves much faster! There are few plateaus or stall-outs with good splitting, and it's very easy to back up a step or move ahead without losing momentum.

Always remember, while the goal may be terribly obvious to *us* ("I want my dog to sit quietly while people walk in the front door"), the learner doesn't necessarily have a clue of what we want or how he can achieve it. Splitting ensures a strong history of success through successive approximations, always moving toward the end goal. This history supports our training even when the learner is confused, distracted, or stressed, and it's important to build it in. When in doubt, break the next step into five smaller steps!

Targeting

I generally start with teaching the dog to "target," or

make physical contact with a designated target, for several reasons:

- 🐾 It's easy! Quick success builds confidence and trust in both dog and handler.
- 🐾 For many dogs, it's their first introduction to analytical thinking — they must move their focus away from the food in the treat bag or hand, to focus on the target, to make the click happen, which produces the food they wanted.
- 🐾 That process above is a microscopic version of the self-control and assessment we want to teach them for the trigger situation.
- 🐾 It's almost never a poisoned cue; no one has ever seized the dog's head and forced it into a target, so it has a clean reinforcement history.

I like to teach dogs to touch their nose (easy and natural) to my hand, as I'll always have it with me — especially important if I'm using targeting to manage a reactive dog. I use two extended fingers as my target, because it doesn't look like any other gestures I'm likely to use throughout the day. (Others like to use an open hand to target the palm, or a single pointed finger, or a closed fist; whatever you choose is fine as long as you are consistent and the dog can consistently distinguish the target from other hand movements.)

With your thumb on the clicker, present your target at nose-height or lower to the dog (without jabbing it at his face). Almost every dog will sniff at it interestedly —

"Hey, you just stuck something out here! Is it cool?" and that gives you a chance to click the nose moving toward the target.

If the dog is grabby about the treats, simply drop one to deliver; don't try to teach two things (targeting and treat manners) at the same time. Be sure to retract your target after the click and then present it again after the dog has finished the treat; there should be a clear start and end to each repetition.

A typical training session should run 30-90 seconds. Resist the urge to push longer, even if you're doing well; that's a great time to stop, before any mistakes happen! When your dog really understands this behavior, you should be completing about 15 target repetitions per minute.

> ## Give yourself a hand
>
> *Hold the clicker in one hand, and the other will be your target. Keep your treats in your clicker hand, in a training pouch, or on a nearby table, not in your target hand; your dog will probably already come toward food, and we don't need to train that!*
>
> *Keep your clicker hand away from the dog, perhaps at your side or behind your back, to keep from confusing him with too many options and to avoid clicking near his face. You don't want the sound to startle him!*

Treat Delivery

Very often I will toss the treat to one side or another for the dog to retrieve as we work. There are several reasons for this, and again, it's all about making this work for us in as many ways as possible.

Movement helps to relieve stress. (Anyone who has ever seen a dog get "the zoomies" during agility or after a bath has seen this in action!) While walking or trotting back and forth after treats generally isn't enough to negate all stress, it can be a great tension reliever, especially with anxious dogs. And by tossing the treat near or far, I can dose out the movement in a controlled fashion and prevent an attack of the zoomies or other stress-venting behavior.

Also, quite a few anxious dogs "get stuck," as I call it — they freeze in place, uncertain of what to do and therefore doing nothing. The longer they remain there, the harder it is to dislodge them and get them moving again, and we can't click an inactive dog! The freeze is also strengthening the underlying anxiety; they can't relax mentally while they're clenched physically. Tossing the treat induces them to move, even a short distance, which keeps them from locking up and "getting stuck."

Additionally, tossing treats gives us good insight into the dog's state of mind. If he grabs his treat and whips around for another repetition, we know he's in an ideal learning mode. If he takes the treat, sniffs about on the floor, looks about the room, and finally turns back to the trainer, that's a pretty good indication that he's stressed, and we probably want to modify the training to make him more successful and more engaged. Simply handing the dog a treat does not give him latitude to respond in different ways.

Finally, we can use treat delivery to emphasize different training points. I might deliver a treat to different parts of the room to set the dog to return at different angles, generalizing the approach to the target, for example. I might treat away from the mat during matwork to reinforce the approach to the mat, and then reward in place on the mat to promote a relaxed posture with no hurry to get up.

Treat in whatever fashion makes your training work better!

Adding a Cue

I could talk for hours about cues — and I have done exactly that — but we're sticking to the basics for right now. When your dog is watching for the target, when you can present it to the right or left, high or low, and know he's going to touch it, and when you can easily achieve 15 target repetitions in a minute, you're ready to add the verbal cue.

A cue is the prompt for a behavior, the "green light" to go ahead and do a trained behavior which now has the opportunity to earn reinforcement. For pet dogs these are most often verbal ("sit") or visual (hand signal).

My quick litmus test, for assessing whether a behavior is ready for a cue, is my famous (infamous!) $50 bet — if you're willing to slap money on the table and say "Watch this! Fifty bucks says he'll nail it, first time!" as you present your target, certain your dog will win the bet for you, you're ready to attach a cue. If you're willing to bet $5, but not $50, you're not ready to use a cue yet!

Why wait to use the cue? There are two very good reasons.

Learned irrelevance is the phenomenon of tuning out data which has no real meaning. A mother will respond to a child's cry of real pain or fear, but she will often ignore fussy sounds or a toddler playfully talking to herself. Because the noise has no significant meaning, she doesn't have to listen for it. In the same way, a dog can ignore "meaningless" human noise which isn't yet attached to a clear concept, and it can be harder to retrain a snappy response to those cues later.

The other reason is that we want good, reliable responses to our cues. If we teach the dog the cue in the earliest stages of the behavior, while the behavior is still uncertain and unreliable, we're associating the cue with that uncertain, unreliable behavior! By waiting until the behavior is solid, we can attach a more solid cue.

Attaching a cue to a target is simple — with your hand neutral and still, say your new cue ("Touch") and *then* present your target. Your dog will touch it, and you will click and treat. (If you are tempted to repeat the word, the delay means he's still having to think about the target behavior, and he's not ready for the cue yet. Practice without a verbal cue until you're ready for the $50 bet!) Repeat until you can see him looking for your hand when you say, "touch."

Those familiar with training might note that this is not full stimulus control, but it's all we need for the moment.

Now practice randomly throughout the day, surprising your dog with "touch" at odd moments. He will be happy to do so (and he should be consistently reinforced).

If you're training in a new place, or with a distraction present, remember that $50 bet — it's perfectly acceptable to review the behavior without the cue word until you're certain he's ready for it! You don't want to practice associating the cue with either frustration or failure, only sweet success.

Settling on a Mat

Now we're going to shape the dog to relax on a mat. Make sure your location is clear of distractions and let's get started.

Even if your dog reliably downs on cue already, it's important to shape this behavior! There are a number of reasons for this:

- 🐾 The shaping dog is working proactively, not reactively
- 🐾 The shaped down is typically more relaxed than the coerced, lured, or prompted downs
- 🐾 The dog is practicing active self-assessment rather than relying upon handler guidance

The process is more important than the position.

Many people are tempted to "help" the dog here by prompting the dog to lie on the mat. Resist! **The process is more important.** Remember, our ultimate goal is not the dog's physical position on the mat, as we will eventually move beyond the mat, but the dog's frame of mind, and prompting him here will actually delay achieving that.

There are multiple steps to the mat-shaping process, and

some dogs will require intermediary steps while others may leap ahead. Be patient and don't worry; the dog's performance here is not an indicator of his long term success! This has far more to do with his previous training experiences, whether he's used to prompting or handler help.

Remember, every click produces a treat. I recommend placing the treats in the center of the mat; it can help dogs focus on the mat instead of the handler's hands, particularly useful if the dogs are not experienced shapers. But food treats are **rewards, not bribes** — they appear on the mat only after the dog performs a behavior, meets criteria, and hears a click!

Be sure to have your thumb on the clicker, ready to go, when you start the session — it's a very common mistake to miss the dog's first orientation to the mat because the handler didn't expect it so soon and wasn't ready.

With the dog watching, place the mat on the floor and:

1. Click for any orientation toward the mat. As with the target, most dogs will look at or sniff the new thing. Be ready, as this can happen while you're still placing the mat!
2. Click for looking at the mat.
3. Click for nose pointing toward the mat.
4. Click for nose moving toward the mat.
5. Click for a sit, if offered, if the dog is still orienting to the mat. If the dog's sit results in staring fixedly

at the handler, back up to step #1 and ignore the sit. (Dogs may skip #5 to jump straight to #7; it often depends on their conformation. Either route is fine!)

6. Click for nose moving down while sitting. (I call this posture The Vulture, sitting and hunching with the muzzle toward the mat.)
7. Click for elbows bending and/or body lowering toward mat. Many dogs will move their front feet as they lower themselves; watch for the front toes to move forward. Click for chest lowering.
8. Click for lying down.

Once the dog is lying, continue to treat, placing food between their front paws. Make this a memorable event — "Ye gads, why on earth didn't I lie down right away? This is awesome!" Remember that **five pennies is way more than a nickel**; many small treats given individually are more powerful than fewer large ones.

When the dog has received ten to twenty treats while lying down, present your target to one side of the mat. (I wouldn't use the verbal cue here yet; your $50 probably isn't safe!) Gently encourage the dog to touch the target, but don't be surprised if he's reluctant; he just got a bazillion treats (by dog reckoning) for being on the mat, so he's likely reluctant to leave it, and he hasn't been thinking about the target. When he does move, click and treat, and then wait.

We are looking for him to recall that the mat was a font of delicious opportunity and to orient to it again, allowing you to start again at step #1. It is *not* your job to direct him to the mat; it is his task to analyze what he was doing to earn all those delightful treats and decide what to do next.

If he hesitates, keep quiet and let him think. Movement or talking on your part will disrupt him. Click the first movement he makes toward the mat, even if it's only with his eyes. (Again, place the treats in the center of the mat *after* the click.)

> ## Not quite right?
>
> ### The dog is looking at me instead of the mat
>
> Most likely, your treat hand is moving early; review your mechanics. Or, you may be staring at the dog; look at the mat, and observe the dog peripherally.
>
> ### The dog is wandering and ignoring the mat
>
> The rate of reinforcement is low, and you may have missed some interactions with the mat. Start over, being sure to click each and every time the dog orients to the mat.

If he really gets stuck and seems to have no idea that the mat is still there, simply pick up the mat and reset for a fresh repetition. This is particularly common in dogs accustomed to handler prompts or direction; it's just a phase of learning the new analytical, proactive skills.

Keep in mind, though, that your training session should be short. Take a break if the dog is losing focus. This can feel like hard work, but it will be worth it!

As you continue, you'll find the dog will start to lie down sooner and sooner each time, recognizing that he might as well get comfortable and the pay is better down there. You'll also see that while his very first down was probably poised to get up again, legs beneath him and muscles ready, his downs will become more and more relaxed. "I'm gonna be here a while, enjoying breakfast in bed; might as well get comfy!"

This is part of what we're cultivating, a relaxed posture and a relaxed mind. It's one reason we did not cue a down here, but let the dog "discover" it himself; we want *only* this association with the mat.

Once the dog is lying down readily on the mat, we're ready to start shaping for relaxation itself. Warm up your clickers! and click any of the following:

- Head lowering to mat, chin resting on leg or mat
- Tail uncurling or resting on floor
- Hip rocking to one side
- Hind legs slipping further from body
- Hind legs extending behind body ("frog legs")
- Sighing
- Blinking and soft eyes
- Ears relaxing
- Rolling onto one side

You get the picture — anything that's an indicator of

relaxation, you can click[10]. It's perfectly acceptable to click for all of these at once; your criterion isn't the action itself but the relaxation producing it. Sometimes, in dogs with slick coats, you can actually watch the shoulder muscles unclench!

It's common for dogs to go through a period of "faking it" — a dog might place his chin on the floor and look at you hopefully, clearly doing it for the treat and not because he's sleepy. That's okay; click and treat anyway. He's still wholly in the proactive frame of mind we want, and like the Velveteen Rabbit, if he keeps pretending, it will become real.

Now that you're clicking for relaxation, don't worry about resetting the dog with a target; we're working on chilling out, not finding the mat. To finish a training session, still target to one side so that the dog leaves the mat and drop a treat, allowing you to collect the mat while the dog finds the treat.

I don't generally add a verbal cue to the mat, because its presence is a cue in itself and because I don't want to be relying on verbal cues later in the process — I want the

---

[10] Some dogs with very strong reinforcement histories may find the clicker itself too arousing to efficiently shape relaxation. My Laevatein was one of these; the click was such a powerfully conditioned reinforcer that it was just too stimulating to synthesize with relaxation. If this is the case, simply introduce a new marker — no need to condition it, just start marking and treating — and use this new marker only for matwork.

> I have worked with anxious or aggressive dogs who would start to relax and then suddenly clench up again — "Oh, I forgot to be worried!" These dogs are chronically stressed in their daily lives, and being "comfortably relaxed" feels uncomfortably strange to them.
>
> If you find this to be the case, just keep clicking for relaxed postures, and little by little their periods of calm will grow longer. If you don't see improvement, check Chapter 12 to see if he might be a candidate for drug therapy.

dog to be able to make decisions based on his environment without the handler's help. So your training sessions should be wholly silent except for praise delivered between the click and the treat.

Continue this until you have a mat addict. This usually takes about a week of several one-minute training sessions a day, but of course dogs vary as much as human students do. Leslie McDevitt in *Control Unleashed* describes dogs leaping into the air to ride a dropped mat to the ground, and I've seen restless dogs reach into their gear bags and pull out their mats so they can lie on them. That's the attitude we're cultivating: If there's a mat to be found, the dog should be chilling on it and he should be getting paid for doing so!

Then you can start moving the mat to various locations, such as each room of the house, introducing mild distractions — but no triggers yet. We're just teaching the dog that the mat might be available anywhere, and it's *always* a good idea to relax on it.

On Poisoned Cues

Now might be a good time to discuss poisoned cues and why we particularly need to avoid them.

A poisoned cue, for our purposes, is any cue which predicts an undesirable or ambiguous outcome for the learner — that is, sometimes the signal ("sit") is followed by positive reinforcement ("Good boy! Here's a treat!"), and sometimes by positive punishment and negative reinforcement (handler presses on dog's hips while pulling up on collar, releasing pressure after dog sits).

Why would this be a problem? Some even advise that using both desired and undesired consequences helps the dog to learn faster and better. While I haven't seen any research to support that, we do have indications that the blend of positive and negative reinforcement can dampen learning and inhibit the learner's enthusiasm.

More importantly for the agitated dog, a poisoned cue introduces more ambiguity and more stress into a scenario, which is exactly what he does *not* need.

A dog who is already having trouble focusing, for any reason, will not be aided by adding more stress. Any signal which carries an implicit threat[11], as a poisoned

---

[11] Remember, the learner is the one to define the severity of the threat. Many humans think physical manipulation of a dog is probably no big deal, compared to pinch collars or electric shock — but to many dogs, particularly anxious dogs, it can be very aversive.

cue does, will of course also carry some stress.

I'm not aware of any definitive research on the subject, but I have seen the same dogs near threshold respond correctly to new, clean cues and lose control at old, poisoned cues.

How do you know if a cue is poisoned? You might see any or all of the following:

- 🐾 The learner is reluctant to begin the training session
- 🐾 The learner shows visible signs of stress in the training session or at the presentation of the cue
- 🐾 Behavior breaks down (increased latency, lower precision, slower speed) following the cue
- 🐾 Behavior breaks down preceding the cue (when the learner can predict the cue is coming)

Because of these effects, while a poisoned cue is still technically a cue and can often still be used as a reinforcer, its use will produce significantly different behavior and, important for us, a significantly different attitude toward the proceedings. As we are trying to reduce a dog's emotional involvement and bring him to a calmer, more rational state of mind, it's not a risk worth taking.

> *A student of mine was demonstrating to a group, and her dog started out doing well, fetching an object each*

Quite often handlers are surprised to learn their cues are poisoned, but the difference in response tells the tale!

time she cued, "Take it!"

As the handler grew nervous in front of others, however, she reverted under stress to previously-learned behavior (yep, humans do that, too!) and used a signal from her previous training days, "Bring," which had been trained with combined positive and negative reinforcement. Immediately the dog lowered his head and flattened his ears, and he performed the behavior more slowly and less reliably, sometimes needing several prompts to complete the exercise.

The student was initially confused by the dog's altered behavior, but she then recognized her own change. She went back to the cue she had retrained with positive reinforcement only, and the dog's performance went back to happy and reliable.

For severe cases of fear or aggression, if I am not wholly certain that the dog's repertoire consists of entirely "clean" cues, we train new cues to the behaviors we're likely to need while working. This is one reason I nearly always start with targeting; it's almost never a poisoned cue! But even everyday behaviors such as "sit" can become more reliable and more calming when there is no ambiguous reinforcement history attached to them.

Chapter 4 Reactive & Proactive

WHAT'S GOING ON
IN THERE?

Sometimes it helps to visualize what might be going on, mentally and behaviorally. Without an actual window into the dog's mind, we must use artificial constructs.

This is how I organize my thoughts on reactivity, to help structure my training plans. This imagery might not work for everyone, and that's fine.

The Too-Friendly Dog

I ring the doorbell, and I know immediately I'm at the right house. I can hear a dog barking frantically inside, and something thumps against the door. A moment later I hear human voices, first reasonable and then chiding and then frustrated. At last the door is opened, and a woman invites me in with an apologetic smile. Behind her, a man is struggling to hold a retriever mix by the collar. The dog is straining forward, gagging against the collar, trying to jump. His eyes have gone slightly pink.

"He's a really good dog," the woman assures me. "He just gets so excited when people come over."

The friendly agitated dog is one of the most neglected.

Often the behavior is tolerated with the excuse that "he's just friendly," and because this dog frequently can settle down after a time (or after being released to greet and cheerfully maul the object of his enthusiasm), he's often assumed to be harmless or even normal[12].

But this isn't normal greeting behavior. If I met a man on the street who was straining to reach me even as someone tried to hold him back, staring intently at me with elevated heart rate and respiration, I'd get away in a hurry and prepare to defend myself. That kind of behavior isn't friendly, it's grounds for a restraining order. (Indeed, this is why many public dog fights are caused by "friendly" dogs.).

It often surprises people that a friendly dog and an aggressive dog share the same fundamental problem. But the issue isn't whether the dog is happy or angry or scared, it's that his arousal — whatever the cause — is overpowering the rest of his mind.

That can sound a bit nutters, so let's look examine this further.

---

[12] The Appendix includes a list of behaviors which can indicate stress in a dog; it's a good idea to compare your dog's behavior against that to see if your excited or friendly dog might in fact be aroused to the point of distress.

The Continuum

Imagine a continuum running between reactive-emotional-limbic and proactive-thoughtful-rational.

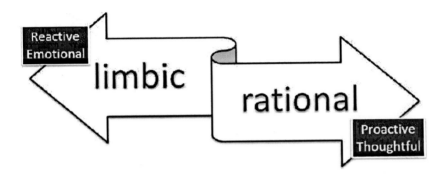

Or, we can define this continuum in more everyday terms....

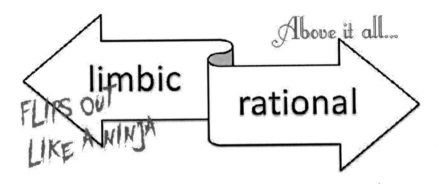

A dog's individual genetics[13] determines the end posts of where it will sit on that continuum. Environment (including training!) then adjusts exactly where a dog

---

[13] It should go without saying, but it bears repeating that while breeds may have general tendencies toward one end of the spectrum or another, breed is *not* a determining factor regarding an individual's temperament or personality.

will rest within those genetic parameters.

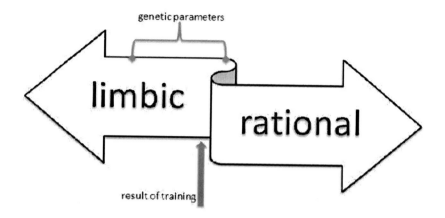

What does this mean? Some dogs just are never going to be very reactive; they're naturally easy-going lugs who are hard to offend and often don't notice everything around them. Other dogs are always going to have a lower threshold and will be challenged by more even in the identical environment. But we can work with (or neglect) those individuals to move them up or down their personal scales.

Additionally, each dog can lean toward one end of the spectrum or another during any given moment. A dog experiencing a panic attack, in full reactive freak-out, has his needle buried at the limbic end.

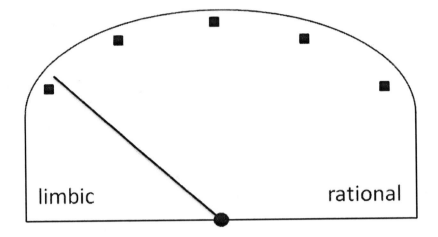

limbic   rational

As we work with the dog, promoting analytical, proactive behavior, that needle will swing toward the other end.

Now, I need to emphasize that none of this is peer-reviewed science; it is merely the referential framework I've developed to explain what I'm observing. If this particular framework doesn't work for you, discard it, no hard feelings. But, practically speaking, we can take this away:

- It is impossible to be reactive and proactive at the same time.
- Dogs already in "limbic mode" (with their needles to the left) have a harder time responding to operant requests — and the dog does not respond reliably to known cues while reacting.
- Dogs already in "rational mode" (with their needles to the right) also have a harder time responding to limbic stimuli — thus a dog busily working with a handler does not respond as

Reactive & Proactive | Fired Up, Frantic, and Freaked Out

quickly or as intensely to a trigger as a dog starting from a neutral state.

The last may sound surprising, because we often don't notice when the dog *doesn't* react, but I see it happen all the time — a dog busily working out a fun training challenge, wholly concentrating on his task, ignores a stimulus which would ordinarily send him into a barking frenzy.

This isn't just for "normal" dogs, either; it's equally true for our agitated dogs.

> *Just a couple of days before I sat down to write this, I had a first lesson with a little pit bull/Dalmatian cross who tended to over-react to outside sights and sounds. As we were working on her very first mat session — her first shaping session ever — a dog began barking outside the front door. This would normally be one of her top triggers!*
>
> *But she only glanced toward the door and then back at the mat, unable to spare the mental energy for a flurry of barking while she was solving the puzzle of how to make us click and treat.*

Her owners were stunned and thrilled, of course! But not only is this common, we'll be counting on it as we move forward.

> *We were introducing a decoy dog, a live trigger, to the little terrier for the first time. A victim of several neighborhood dog attacks, she had learned that the best defense was a good offense, and it had become deeply*

ingrained habit to the point that her owner went to great lengths to keep her from sighting other dogs.

Not only did she ignore the decoy dog to a degree that her handler thought she was unable to see him, she surprised us all when a third dog came unexpectedly barking into the space, straining at the end of his leash, a perfect trigger — and she simply looked at her handler with an expectant gaze, waiting for her opportunity to perform her alternate behavior. She was so immersed in her rational, puzzle-solving mind that it was too difficult to return to her reactive mode.

Now, we won't always have to have the dog actively working to reap this benefit. What the mind practices more often is stronger and more fluent. You know already that rehearsing reactivity makes the behavior stronger (and makes thinking rationally more difficult); it's equally true that rehearsing thoughtful behavior makes reactivity more difficult — which is exactly what we want!

Therefore we want the brain to be practicing proactive, operant thinking. This means that all clicker training — even "stupid pet tricks" — can work toward reducing overall reactivity. So when you take breaks from our formal matwork and related training, go play with some fun tricks; you'll still be working toward your goal!

Predictability and a Sense of Control

An ability to predict how an encounter will go and a sense of control of one's environment are two very key components to confidence. I think many agitated dogs are reacting in an uncomfortable state of limbo, receiving neither behavioral direction nor feedback.

While we want these dogs to learn to self-assess and act proactively, in the meantime the target or other known behaviors can be used to give the dog a deliberate and known behavior to perform with an expectation of reinforcement — touch the handler's or guest's hand for a click and treat, for example, or whatever might be an appropriate level.

A sense of control is especially critical for nervous or fearful dogs. Even if the situation itself is unchanged, the mere idea of control influences the dog's perception of it.

For a human example, consider a trip to the dentist. No one really enjoys it, but most of us can tolerate it — in large part because we control it. We make the decision to go despite our disinclination, we drive ourselves to the clinic, we put ourselves in the chair, and we talk with the hygienist, free to ask for a break or a change in procedure if necessary.

Now imagine that as you walked into the clinic, two men took your arms, pressed you into a dental chair, and locked shackles about your wrists to hold you in place and prevent you from pushing away the hygienist. Then the same hygienist came and performed the same procedure. How is your attitude different? Even if the hygienist is cheerful and smiling, do you feel as secure as when you had the option to move freely?

It takes very little, only a change in human approach, to give an anxious dog a reassuring sense of choice and control. But it can make an enormous difference.

Brain Chemistry and Predictability

There's a chemical reason, too; the brain produces dopamine (the "feel-good" neurotransmitter, for our quick reference) at the presentation of a known cue or stimulus leading to an opportunity for reinforcement — more so than at the presentation of a reinforcer earned after that same cue or stimulus[14]. The learning brain is pleased more by the predictable anticipation of a reward than by the reward itself[15].

Consider also the SEEKING circuit, described by neuroscientist Jaak Panksepp, which is a phenomenon in the hypothalamus which excites the brain to explore its options. It is the opposite number to the brain's reactive alarm system in the amygdala (remember our continuum?) and is maintained most strongly not by

---

[14] Sapolsky, Robert. "Are Humans Just Another Primate?" California Academy of Sciences, Pritzker Lecture. San Francisco, California. 15 February 2011.

[15] This is probably another reason why an agitated dog which will not take food may still respond to known cues. It is obviously important to then present the earned reinforcer, even if the dog does not wish to eat at that moment; the prediction must continue to be accurate!

great rewards, but by small reinforcers earned at irregular intervals[16] — tailor-made for clicker training!

Put another way, the dog learning to sit for treats gets higher brain buzzes off both the cue to "sit" and the resulting click than the following treat.

Framing the trigger within a predictable structure which the dog can influence literally creates a calmer, happier brain chemistry. And that's exactly what we're after.

---

[16] Pryor, Karen. *Reaching the Animal Mind*. New York City: Scribner, 2009. Print.

Chapter 5 Adding a Trigger

CALM, HAPPY, ENTHUSIASTIC —
THIS IS WHAT WE WANT TO SEE!

By this time, your dog is a mat addict. As soon as you bring out the mat, he drops happily on it, relaxed and smiling and waiting for his treat.

Now we're ready to pit the strong reinforcement history of the mat against a carefully-controlled trigger. Make sure your mat is really addictive before you begin!

Trigger, meet Mat; Mat, meet Trigger

There are two ways of proceeding from this point.

The first is to introduce the trigger while the dog is already on the mat. I usually use this approach when teaching door-crazed dogs to relax while someone knocks and enters. It is easier for dogs to maintain calm than to choose it in the moment.

The second is to present the mat and the trigger at the same time and allow the dog to make a choice between reaction and relaxation. I don't use this method until I'm very sure of my foundation work — but it can be very effective for demonstrating a dog's options in the face of a trigger!

For the purposes of discussion, we will start with the easier option and progress to the more difficult.

Introducing a Trigger to the Mat

For the sake of example we'll walk through this process in detail with a barking, jumping, hyper-enthusiastic door-rushing greeter, whom we'll call Beaver, though the concept is the same with any form or expression of over-arousal. This is just an example, and there can be many correct approaches, but this is fairly typical.

Let's look at Beaver's first day practicing with a trigger.

The First Session

First, place the mat and review. Beaver should be all over this by now, happily flopping on his mat and waiting with doggie grin for his reinforcement. He can do this in every room of the house and even on the back deck if the neighbor dogs aren't out. (We haven't tried it with the other dogs out, yet, lest he make a mistake.)

Now, with Beaver settled on the mat, choose a neutral fixture, such as a kitchen cabinet or pantry, and knock once. This might be as light and faint as a simple knuckle rap. Click and treat immediately, *before* Beaver has a chance to stir if he's so inclined.

If the dog fails — stands or moves off the mat — remain absolutely still. Resist the urge to help him back onto the mat. (If Beaver has run to a door or window, barking, then you did not do a single light knock on a neutral surface! Cheaters never prosper.)

If he stands or steps off the mat and then hesitates, looking confused, let him work on the problem. "Did I hear something? I thought I heard something. But no one else seems to be reacting…. Oh, weren't we doing the mat thing?"

When he returns to the mat, click and treat. (This will change shortly, but for now, click and treat his return.) Shape him back down on the mat and treat several times in place for a calm down. Then, knock once, lightly, and click before he can get up.

If Beaver remains on the mat after the knock, but stiffens or barks, go ahead and click and

Splitting Criteria, Splitting Triggers

Why a cabinet or closet? We're splitting our criteria and giving the dog a better chance of success. We know that a knock on the front door will send him over the edge; why set him up to fail? The front door is an emotional hot spot, while no one has ever come out of the kitchen cabinet. It's easier for him to get it right — and remember how to do it right.

On the other hand, what if he jumps up and barks at the sound of the knock? That is why you knock a single time, lightly — and if the knock itself is too challenging for the dog, imagine if we had combined it with the front door, too!

treat — our criteria at this time is just to lie on the mat, and he's done that! Don't worry that you're reinforcing the stiffening or barking; it may feel wrong, but it will work in the end.

What sane dog would be anywhere other than lying on this mat?!

Continue knocking and clicking and treating, observing Beaver's behavior. Most dogs will begin to ignore the knock or even begin to view it as an antecedent to the click and treat. This is what we want (though most dogs won't achieve this in the first short session). Keep your rate of reinforcement high — at the level of, *what sane dog would be anywhere other than on this mat?!* After a minute or so, end the session.

A few dogs will become progressively more agitated. These dogs have a much stronger history with the trigger (knocking), and the repetition is weighting the difficulty. If you see Beaver growing more tense instead of more relaxed, leave off the knocking and go back to clicking for relaxation. Slip in one super-quiet knock for every five to ten clicks for calm. Then end the session.

Short Sessions

Why end here? Because it's going well! Remember that we can always increase the difficulty of an exercise as we move forward; it's at best inefficient and at worst counter-productive to have to back up after a mistake.

> *Every time the dog succeeds, he adds a memory of the right behavior; every time he errs, he adds a memory of the wrong behavior.*

Every time the dog succeeds, he adds a memory of the right behavior and confidence in reinforcement; every time he errs, he adds a memory of the wrong behavior and an additional dose of frustration. Take such small baby steps that the dog can't help but succeed, and you'll make much faster progress than with fewer, larger, stumbling steps!

An Increase in Criteria

In your next training session, we're going to require something else of Beaver. Thus far he has been clicked for going to the mat at the beginning of a session and for returning after any mistakes. That's about to change.

Technically, if a dog leaves the mat, returns to the mat, and receives a click and a treat, all his behavior has been reinforced, including the error of leaving the mat. In the beginning we click for returning to the mat because *go to the mat* was our starting criterion. As we progress and build duration, however, many dogs discover that getting off the mat and back on produces a higher rate of reinforcement than simply waiting for the next click and treat for staying on the mat. And who can blame them for gaming a flawed system?

So we will no longer click the dog for returning to the

mat; our criteria has been raised to *lie calmly on the mat*. If the dog leaves the mat, simply wait for him to return, and then give him another opportunity to earn a click. In other words, you'll reward Beaver for going to the mat by letting him hear a knock and earn a treat.

Chapter 6 The Trigger
– Phase Two

LAEV LOVES TO
CAMP HER MAT!

Notice that we say "phase two" instead of "session two;" each dog will progress differently, and while I could provide averages, that might not be an appropriate guideline for your individual. Check your data — when Beaver is successful (remains lying calmly on the mat) at least 80% of the time, you are ready to move on. (You *were* keeping data, weren't you?)

You're going to add one knock at a time to this exercise, or a smidge of volume at a time, building up to a typical door knock. But it's all going to continue to take place in another room of the house, well away from the emotional hot spot of the front door. We're looking for the dog to hear the knock and look expectantly at you for his treat, lying calmly on the mat without tap dancing, barking, or otherwise betraying agitation.

When I am working in person with a client, I am usually doing the knocking and the clicking, and the owner is delivering the treat. I know we have the dog right where we want him when I can knock and the dog's response is to look expectantly at his owner, away from me and the knocking, looking for the treat.

When you can knock vigorously on the pantry door and your dog just smiles with that smug, "You can't fool me! Where's my cookie?" expression, at least 80% of the time, you're ready to move on.

Expanding the Trigger

So Beaver doesn't think a knock at the pantry door is a big deal? Fantastic. Now we're going to ask him to tolerate a little more from that pantry.

Keep an eye on your click/treat mechanics! It's common here to see the treat hand starting to move before or with the click, instead of after a short pause. Keep your four-beat delivery clean.

If the treat hand sneaks ahead, the dog often learns not to lie calmly during the knock, but to lie calmly while a human visibly delivers food. This can obviously lead to setbacks later, when the handler is not immediately beside the mat or handling food!

Without knocking, jiggle the pantry doorknob. Most likely, nothing will happen, and you can click and treat Beaver for remaining calmly on the mat. Dogs who have been sensitized to the sound of a doorknob as well as a knock, however, might well tense at this new development. Again, if the dog comes off the mat, simply be still and wait for him to return. If he remains on the mat, click and treat, and continue until he is relaxed.

Keep your sessions just a minute or two in length as you gradually add more difficulty, opening the pantry door an inch, then two inches, then three. When you can swing the pantry door wide and Beaver lies calmly on the mat (no barking or shuffling) at least 80% of the time, we're ready to progress.

Move It

This next level will take little additional time, but it's an important intermediate step for many dogs. Move the mat to new locations in the house, settling the dog in any room while you knock on or open the medicine cabinet, the shower door, the coat closet, the utility room door, etc.

You'll want to some distance between you and the mat, as well. Remember to add just one new criterion at a time, so start with a single step away without any knocking, click, and then return to deliver the treat. I usually place the treat right between his paws on the mat, emphasizing his calm, relaxed position on the mat.

If Beaver stands up when you move away, just stand still; he'll realize there was no click! If you've done your work thus far, he'll likely go right back to the mat and lie down to restart the game. Make your next step smaller. (Also, be sure that you are always ending your training sessions with a target or other ending instruction, rather than walking away from the mat!)

Keep an eye on your data; if Beaver doesn't stick to the mat at least 80% of the time as you move, break your training down into smaller steps and just work on that, without any knocking, for a bit. We've got the time.

When he's solid on his mat despite both movement and knocking, graduate toward the front entry of the house (or wherever Beaver's particular hot spot may be), where you can start knocking on the wall beside the front door. Click after the knock, and then return to treat on the mat. If Beaver remains on the mat during the knocking, but stands after the click, go ahead and treat (delivering to the mat regardless of where the dog is), but recognize you're pushing his threshold and it might be best to go back a step.

Continue until you can knock near the front door, and Beaver looks just as relaxed and happily expectant as he did in the kitchen beside the pantry.

Adding the Real Trigger

Thus far, we've been presenting distractions which are mere shadows of the real thing. Just as a vaccine is a weakened form of the disease, we've been presenting weakened forms of the trigger. But because we've done this, the dog is better prepared for exposure to the actual trigger.

Whenever we raise one criterion, we relax others.

Therefore when we first knock at the front door, we are going to knock once, lightly, instead of knocking vigorously as we've been doing at the pantry. Also, you're going to knock at the *inside* of the door — letting the dog see you do it, just as before. The only difference now is the door itself.

Most dogs will grow a bit tense with the added criteria of the hot front door itself. If he remains on the mat, click and treat; remember that we've relaxed all other criteria. If he stands, wait until he lies down again, and then knock once lightly for another opportunity. If he comes off the mat in a flurry of barking, go back to knocking on other surfaces, and try knocking on several different walls, cabinets, and windows before trying the front door again. Your data probably shows that Beaver wasn't quite at 80% success yet.

Some dogs will face a terrible internal conflict when they hear these first knocks at the front door, and I confess it never ceases to be a sadistic sort of funny to me. They feel an obligation to bark, due to years of ingrained door reactivity, and yet they are too happy playing the mat game and really can't be bothered to work themselves into a lather. This often results in a hilarious half-hearted *woof* while watching the handler for a treat.

You might be tempted to withhold the click, thinking that you don't want to reinforce barking, but go ahead

 The Trigger — Phase Two | Fired Up, Frantic, and Freaked Out

and click and treat anyway. The lame bark is a residual symptom, and as the dog progresses it will soon fade entirely. If you reinforced calm, quiet behavior in your initial mat training, it will reassert itself here. (Another reason we worked to teach perfect mat behavior before ever introducing the trigger!)

Withholding the click, however, would frustrate the dog and betray his faith in the mat game, setting him up for trouble when we increase criteria.

Gradually rebuild your criteria until you can knock firmly on the inside of the front door and Beaver can remain calmly on the mat at least 80% of the time.

What About Mistakes?

I have a personal rule of thumb which has no basis in the scientific literature, but which has served me very well for this kind of work.

> If the dog makes a mistake, that's an opportunity to self-assess and self-correct. Dogs have only one way to ask a question, and that is to try it and see what the result is.
>
> If the dog makes the same mistake twice in a row, he clearly couldn't learn from the first mistake, and I have over-faced the dog with a scenario he's not yet ready to meet.

By this guideline, if the dog stands once, realizes his error when I don't click, and remains lying on the mat for the next repetition, he is learning. If he stands, returns to the mat, and then stands again at the next knock, then he's obviously not absorbing the feedback and I am presenting more challenge than he's ready to face. His mistakes are my fault, and it's my job to get him back in the groove at a more appropriate level of criteria.

This is one reason I am very particular about letting the dog self-assess and determine his own behavior; I do not use no-reward markers, and I do not prompt the dog to return to the mat. Doing so muddies the information for both the dog (making the binary click/no-click into a confusing mess of verbal input) and the trainer (is the dog going to the mat because he understands the exercise or because I'm helping him?).

Quite often a client assures me that the dog understands the exercise better because of verbal correction or prompting — but we find with testing the dog has learned to wait for human help, or has learned to perform another behavior in order to nudge the human into giving the cue to go to the mat. Neither of these is what we want!

"Shut up and let the dog think."

As tempting as it is to "help" the dog, and as difficult as it is for many trainers to remain still and quiet, I find we make more reliable progress, with fewer

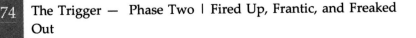

setbacks, if we keep our training simple and clean.

Bringing It All Together

We tend to think of "someone at the front door" as a single trigger stimulus, but the fact is that there are probably many components to that trigger, any of which might normally send Beaver into an agitated reaction.

Just as a storm-fearing dog might fear any of several of the individual aspects of lightning, thunder, pressure change, electrostatic changes, or rain, a dog charging the front door might be triggered by smaller associated sounds or sights.

Now we're ready to desensitize Beaver to all the other pieces of someone coming to the front door. Introduce each of these, one at a time, until Beaver is 80% reliable with all.

- Car engine or car door outside
- Front door handle rattle
- Sound of the security bolt
- The *pop* of the door seal breaking
- The squeak of the hinges
- The owner calling, "Just a minute, I'm coming"
- The sight of someone at the window
- The sound of a knock outside the door
- The doorbell (may require a separate introductory session just as the knocking did)
- The beep of an alarm system
- The door opening (again, one inch at a time)

🐾 Anything else which might be applicable

I have worked with dogs who would, before training, fly into a frenzy at just the sound of the hinges or the slide of the security bolt, both of which were associated with people's arrival. These mini-triggers needed to be introduced on their own before the dogs could be successful at the front door.

A Two-Way Conversation

With particularly difficult challenges, dogs may need some extra time to settle and prepare themselves for the trigger. This is probably exactly like what happens when I go to the optometrist and need to mentally prepare myself before the technician presses that intimidating device against my eyeball.

I am particularly sensitive about my eyes, and if the technician comes too quickly or before I am ready, I will flinch away — or think of defensive actions. If I have a moment to prepare myself, on the other hand, we can complete the examination without an unsettling display of fear or human aggression!

It can be very helpful, in some cases, to give the dog a way to indicate if he's ready for the presentation of the trigger. I stumbled upon this concept while working to desensitize my Laevatein to gunfire, which had previously sent her into panic; together we developed a conversation in which she could indicate to me, by placing her chin fully on the mat, that she was ready for the trigger. I could then present the stimulus (a cap gun, at that point), mark her continued down on the mat, and reinforce.

If she did not put her chin on the mat, I simply waited for her to be ready. She was in complete control of whether or not the cap gun was fired.

If I had to wait more than a few seconds, I knew I was

pushing too fast; in this case, criteria was for *her* to cue *me* (to present the trigger) within a certain period of time.

About a year ago I spoke with Emelie Johnson Vegh, who was using this concept with Eva Bertilsson in their excellent agility program to teach prospects to enjoy noise and motion. They called it an "initiator cue," a cue from the dog to the human that the dog is ready for the stimulus.

It is, in fact, the dog's *request* for the trigger stimulus, in order to earn reinforcement.

The Importance of Choice

Again, it is critical throughout the entire process that the dog be the one making all the decisions and feel he has a choice. Predictability and choice are key to helping a dog be relaxed and calm. We do not fear what we control.

Initiator cues, while not always necessary, are just one additional way for the dog to feel he can predict and has some control of his environment. If your agitated dog is facing a difficult challenge, consider utilizing one.

Inertia and Momentum

This seems like a great deal of training, but the good news is, each successive trigger typically progresses much more quickly, as the dog is simultaneously slipping further to the rational end of the spectrum and learning how this particular game works.

And yes, I encourage clients to think of it as a game. "Can you chill on your mat even if…?" This light-hearted approach keeps both dogs and handlers relaxed.

Remember, many dogs have not only their innate reactions to the trigger, but months or years of associated human emotion, as well. "Every time someone comes to the front door, Mum and Dad get really angry and yell at me! I *hate* when people come to the front door!"

This process can actually move quite rapidly. Many of my private clients see their dogs go from a knock at the pantry door to me walking in the front door in roughly an hour's session (comprised of many tiny training sessions with frequent breaks). We take many, many baby steps, but with so little room for error, progress is steady and reliable. It's not uncommon to hear something like, "We just made more progress in one hour than in three years of working on this."

> *"We just made more progress in one hour than in three years of working on this."*

That "miracle" is due to the fact that the dogs were already familiar with and eager to play the mat game, and criteria was split finely enough[17] that very few mistakes occurred as we worked through the levels. Precise splitting can make a progression in criteria nearly invisible, so there is hardly any challenge moving from one to the next. Of course

---

[17] A colleague once called me the Queen of Splitting, and it is one of my favorite compliments ever!

there's more training to go as well, but now the owner has seen what's possible and has a protocol to follow.

If your training doesn't move quite that quickly, don't worry![18] You might need to split a little more finely, or you might need to work in shorter sessions with more frequent breaks, or you might have a dog who needs a little more time.

You should see steady improvement, though; the advantage of so many tiny steps is that there are no plateaus to stall your progress!

---

[18] Professional trainers can often work faster because they have years of experience to draw upon. If both you and your dog are newer to this approach, it only makes sense that it might take a bit longer.

Chapter 7   Off the Mat

WORKING IN THE ZONE!

While I like to start matwork first, because it is a fantastic foundation for the dog who needs to learn he actually has choices in how to respond to stimuli, it's obvious not all our training can take place on the mat.

Some dogs graduate off the mat as they become more proficient at coping and can wean away the crutch; some dogs work simultaneously on the mat and off, in different training plans.

> *This wasn't Laev's first obedience trial, but she was still young, only a couple of years old. We entered the ring and set up at the start of the heeling pattern, and the judge approached. "This will be the heel on-leash. Are you ready?"*
>
> *"Yes, ma'am, we're ready."*
>
> *Laev, sitting raptly at heel, began to chatter her teeth, still watching me. The judge looked down at her. "Um, is she okay?"*
>
> *"She's fine. She's just eager to work."*
>
> *"If you say so.... Forward."*

Not all dogs who are losing their sanity to their emotions are fearful or in distress — many are legitimately thrilled to be doing what they love best! But it is possible for them to be both happy and intense in their work without being frantic, and ultimately this makes them better sport dogs who learn more quickly and perform more reliably.

It is my firm belief that clicker dogs[19] are better prepared to learn while in arousal. *Arousal itself is not the enemy* — it's the loss of conscious or rational thought which we want to avoid. A dog who is excited and intense while fully cognitive is our ideal!

Not sure what I mean, or if that's even possible, much less preferable? Let's look at it another way.

Action!

Imagine, for a moment, that we are auditioning canine actors for heroes in a daring new summer action movie. We need to find the perfect lead, a Bruce Lee or Lucy Liu of dogdom.

The first candidate is full of passion and fire, loud and fast and strong. Unfortunately, she isn't accurate, and she wastes a great deal of energy in surplus movement, her constant shouting makes it difficult for the director to direct or even to concentrate, and her constant muscle

---

[19] By this I mean dogs who regularly practice shaping exercises, who are practiced at thinking analytically in the moment.

tension actually makes her reactions slower and less effective. She looks impressive at a casual glance, but she's easy to trip up. The martial arts consultants shake their heads in disdain.

The second candidate has none of the previous hopeful's uncontrolled frenzy, and he's technically correct in his movements, but he may be in fact a bit too relaxed; his kicks look lazy, his punches barely connect, and his flips are downright anemic. The producers imagine a disappointed and outraged audience, and they give the thumbs down.

The third candidate walks calmly to the audition stage, but there's just something about her.... She begins her *kata*, and each movement is mathematical, precise, and deadly. She exudes concentration and grace. She is all intensity and power, balance and ferocity, spirit and accuracy. She is Yun-Fat Chow, Jackie Chan, and Jet Li all neatly packaged up with Lee van Cleef and Chuck Norris, and she has barely completed her routine when contracts are flourished for her attention.

We want the third candidate.

The Illusion of "Protective"

Sometimes clients tell me they actually like their dogs being hectic. "I *want* him to bark when someone's at the door," is a common statement. "That's an advantage of having a dog!"

True! And my living conditions are such that I prefer my Dobermans to bark when someone approaches the house, too. But there's a significant difference between a dog choosing to bark to alert me of strangers, and a dog needing to bark because he is unsettled by the strangers.

Almost always when a dog is described as "protective" we find the dog is actually anxious or displaying fear-aggression. This is easily identified by observing whether or not the dog can settle as quickly as the human. A dog who continues to hackle, bark, or otherwise "guard" the house or owner is a dog who is afraid; a dog who has assessed a lack of threat relaxes promptly and enjoys the new company.

"Wouldn't you prefer your dog to bark when someone comes to the door and then also be able to settle quietly once you've identified and welcomed whoever it is?"

"Yes, actually, that'd be perfect! But can we have both barking and calm?"

Yes, we can. By teaching the dog to be thoughtful and to assess the situation, we can have a dog who identifies when alert barking is necessary but does not panic or overreact and can therefore settle quickly. Best of both worlds.

"Power is Nothing Without Control"

This phrase, for years the Pirelli Tires™ sales slogan, was constantly on my mind as I worked out training plans for Laevatein. I wanted intensity, but I wanted reliable control, but I wanted intensity.

Again, it's possible to have both.

Here are some training points to keep in mind as you work away from the mat and particularly in any sport work.

Split Finely

I know, I know, we've covered this splitting thing before! But I can't emphasize it enough. When I coach someone who is struggling with twenty steps of focused heeling, I may soon have them clicking for a single step. This can feel very backward and frustrating to the handler — but the difference in the dog soon alleviates that, as the clearer criteria and resulting higher rate of reinforcement create a more stable, more reliable behavior.

How do you know where to set your criteria? Let your dog show you what the cue means to him now.

Cue once.

Repeating cues is a very common mistake, but it's one of the more dangerous ones, capable of misdirecting even the dedicated trainer's attention.

Imagine an agility start line stay, in which the handler reminds the dog, "Stay... stay... stay," as he moves away. Or a protection routine, in which the handler cues, "Heel, wait, heel," as the team approaches the decoy. The dog may be visibly agitated, but he performs the behavior, and so the handler assumes all is well.

All is not well! The agility dog does not have a start line stay for the duration of the handler's lead-out, only for the brief interval between "stay" cues. The protection sport dog does not know to hold heel position while approaching the supreme distraction, only how to return to it when reminded. And there is a big difference between these "Band-Aid™ behaviors," as I call them, and clean, reliable behavior.

Worse, because the dog did appear to perform correctly, the *handler's* behavior was reinforced as well. (Training works both ways!) The act of repeating cues or otherwise assisting the dog will become stronger, and it will be harder to train clean, reliable behavior.

The solution is to cue once. If the dog needs a second cue after five feet of heeling, the solution is not to cue again, but to extend the dog's concept of duration heeling. Repeating the cue — or helping in other, more subtle ways, such as body blocks, leash prompts, etc. — only muddies the data on the dog's understanding and creates bad habits in the handler.

If the dog appears to need additional cues — if the handler is tempted to use additional cues to prop up a sagging behavior not yet able to take the strain of this scenario — split or reduce criteria until the dog can be successful on a single cue, and build from there.

Just as in previous exercises, the dog must make his own decisions and show us the behavior he knows, without prompting or assistance. "Helping" him only slows the actual progression toward finished behavior.

Consider also if alternate sources of reinforcement are giving the dog contradictory feedback.

Don't Accidentally Reinforce Unwanted Behavior

I watched a team heel toward a protection blind, the dog trying to surge ahead to reach the incredibly valuable decoy inside. The handler was in clear conflict with the dog, and they argued all the way to the blind: "Heel! Heel! Heel!"

What was actually happening here?

- If the cue "heel" were trained positively, it was a tertiary reinforcer[20], approximately the same value as a click — and every repetition of "heel!" was in

---

[20] A positively-trained (not poisoned) cue predicts an opportunity for positive reinforcement. Cue → click → reinforcer, so just as the click is a secondary reinforcer, a cue is a tertiary reinforcer. (This is what makes behavior chains so wonderful!)

effect clicking and reinforcing the dog's leaving position.

☙ Since the dog wanted to get closer to the blind, each step forward was a reinforcer for behavior the handler did not want.

Consequently, no matter how much effort the handler put into controlling and correcting the dog, the behavior did not improve!

Judicious dispensing of reinforcement and splitting, however, can solve this in a much less frustrating way:

☙ Split criteria to a single heeling step at a time. Mark and reinforce with access to the decoy.

☙ If the dog surges ahead, abort the rep instead of trying to correct it. Reset and start fresh, so that no errors are included in any reinforcement.

☙ If the dog surges ahead twice[21], reconsider; the dog has just informed us that he does not understand or is not yet capable of meeting this criterion.

☙ For maximum effect, consider back-chaining the heeling approach — that is, starting just one step away from the decoy[22], then two, then three, etc.

---

[21] See "What About Mistakes?" on page 73.

[22] There are many ways to manipulate the power of a distraction, and if being near the decoy is too much for the dog, start close to the decoy but with the decoy facing away, for example. Reduce criteria until the dog can be successful — then make it harder, one clean step at a time.

Handlers might not like the idea of going backward so far; after all, who wants to progress from twenty steps of heeling to one? But in reality, they didn't have twenty steps of heeling; they'd only blurred the fact that they had just one or two.

All Dogs Can Be Reliable

This isn't just for sport dogs, either; chants of "stay, stay, stay!" are just as common in the pet world. But it's not hard to create clean, reliable behavior with "pet manners," either — and of course the dogs don't know the difference between silly pet tricks or competitive sport or serious life-saving work; they just know what behavior is worth doing.

Chapter 8 Adding a Mat to the Trigger

CHOOSE YOUR HAPPY PLACE,
CHOOSE YOUR HAPPY PLACE....

The second method of using matwork to help a dog through a trigger situation is to present the mat alongside the trigger, inviting the dog to choose between the well-conditioned mat and emotional reaction, rather than allowing the dog to simply continue a relaxed behavior already in progress.

This is more challenging to the dog, requiring an active decision rather than inertia, and I do not choose this approach unless I know the dog is prepared. It's a gamble, of course, but this is my card game and I will stack the deck to my favor.

If we prepare the training scenario properly, and the dog experiences early success and powerful reinforcement, we can see evidence of a really amazing phenomenon.

> *An operant conditioned response will kick in before the adrenaline surge.... Operant Conditioning works at the speed of nerve,*

Adding a Mat to the Trigger | Fired Up, Frantic, and Freaked Out

hormones at the speed of blood.[23]

Rory Miller wrote that in relation to self-defense, but it is true in other situations as well — and don't forget that the motivation for many reactive dogs *is* self-defense. Instead of programming an effective physical defense, here we are installing self-interruption and alternate behavior.

For the sake of example, we will talk though this process with a typical subject whom we'll call Dozer. Let's say that Dozer, determined that the best defense is a good offense, has dragged his owners down sidewalks and across streets to rage at other dogs. We want to teach him to interrupt his own reaction and to relax in the presence of other dogs.

Preparation

Again, we will create a scenario which gives the Dozer the best chance at making the decision we want him to make. We're going to make it very easy for him to be right!

- 🐾 Dozer will already be a mat addict, flopping happily on the mat as soon as it appears without hesitation or prompting.
- 🐾 I have enlisted a decoy dog to serve as trigger whom I can trust to ignore Dozer even if Dozer

---

[23] Miller, Rory (2011-04-01). *Facing Violence: Preparing for the Unexpected* (p. 103).

barks or lunges. My decoy dog handler is similarly unflappable and will ignore Dozer as necessary.

🐾 I have identified a location which allows me to present and remove the decoy dog at will[24], with enough distance to provide a fair starting criterion.

🐾 For dogs who have displayed aggression, I often have a second collar and line (both rated for protection work) secured as a safety net around a tree or post. The dog's everyday collar and leash are in the hands of his handler, as usual. We shouldn't need the backup equipment, but precaution doesn't hurt — and often knowing a safety net exists allows humans to relax further, too, which only helps Dozer.

This may seem like a lot of preparation, but I get only one first opportunity, and I want Dozer to make the right decision! As with the previous method, I want to take many successful steps to build memory, new habit, and a seamless momentum of success.

Getting Started

Once Dozer is settled in our chosen location, on leash

---

[24] Especially for longer distances, a phone and headset can be very useful here. Connect the call and leave it open throughout the session, so each handler can hear the other. This eliminates the need for raising the voice or gesturing, both of which can add intensity to Dozer's situation and by varying the words which request the decoy dog's appearance, Dozer's prediction of the decoy dog can be avoided, giving a true picture of just his reactions.

with his handler and also secured with our backup equipment, he gets to warm up doing behaviors he knows well — a little bit of matwork, lots of targeting and any other un-poisoned cues. We aren't going to throw the choice at him cold; he's already going to be thinking when he first sees the new puzzle.

This is a place to use very high value treats — combat pay, you might call them! This is going to be a lot of effort for Dozer, and we want him to be certain that it's worth it. I tend to wear my treats in an easily-accessible wide-mouth bag[25] on my waist, with the leash handle slid over my wrist and through my hand so I can hold it without the risk of dropping it. The mat is under my arm, rolled and tucked into my back waistband, or nearby behind me (not on the ground). Get comfortable with the pieces as you warm up with Dozer, and wait until you and Dozer are both ready before moving ahead.

When he's happily working, and while the mat is put away, we cue the decoy dog to enter at a distance beyond what Dozer's reactivity zone is known to be[26]. The decoy dog is visible but calm, standing still or lying down and

---

[25] You never want your food delivery delayed by cramped pockets or clinging plastic baggies; practice in advance so you know you can dish out those treats quickly!

[26] This distance is determined by Dozer's history, not by what we humans think it *should* be. For some dogs this can be a hundred feet or so — that's fine. The distance will get shorter. What's important is that Dozer can get it right in the beginning.

facing directly away from Dozer; this makes him minimally obtrusive or threatening. We watch for Dozer to notice.

When Dozer sees the decoy dog, he will go still, lifting his head and stiffening. But the decoy dog is far enough, and still enough, that Dozer needs just a second to decide if and how he's going to react, or perhaps even to decide if that really is a dog over there.

At that precise moment, *before* Dozer can react, we visibly present the mat.

There is no verbal cue, no prompting, no attempt to interfere with Dozer's view of the decoy dog. He must make a choice, *on his own*, between barking at the strange dog and going to his mat.

If we have set up our scenario correctly, Dozer will look at his mat and go to it[27]. Click and treat immediately, even before he reaches it or lies down, if he's at all slow. That's fine — with an increase in criteria (strange dog), other criteria (latency in lying down on the mat) may be relaxed. Shape Dozer all the way onto the mat if necessary, if he does not lie down immediately on his own, placing the treats on the mat exactly as usual.

---

[27] I have even seen some dogs greet the mat with apparent relief — "Oh, thank God, my mat! Now I don't have to deal with that other thing!"

Once Dozer is on the mat, continue to treat as the decoy dog quietly disappears from view, with as little disturbance as possible.

What Just Happened?

From Dozer's perspective, he was working and earning treats — all well and good — when a strange dog showed up. But it was really far away, and not looking at him, not even moving, really, and so while he was trying to decide what to do about it, his mat appeared. Ah, the mat! He loves the mat. He went to it, still wondering about the other dog, and earned delicious treats for every stage of mat-work. And as he settled on the mat, recalling just how much he loved this game, and how much easier it was than getting all riled up, the scary dog went away.

> *Once the dog has made the decision — and learned he can make that decision — we have what we need. The rest is mere extension.*

The mat — and its associated calm — was both positively and negatively reinforced. More importantly, Dozer interrupted his own arousal and chose the mat over barking.

That is the critical point. Now the rest is just a matter of degrees!

Chapter 9 Adding the Mat – Phase Two

"THE MAT IS MY SECURITY BLANKET. REALLY."

The critical decision has been made; we know it's possible for Dozer to interrupt his own aroused reaction (even if just in the very earliest stages) and choose an alternate behavior.

Now we must convince Dozer that he is in fact capable of doing that every time, and that it's always the most worthwhile and safest option. The key, again, is careful splitting, so that it's always easiest for Dozer to make the choice we want him to make.

Carry on!

Split It Fine

Just as with introducing a collection of triggers to the dog on the mat, we must split our trigger components and criteria very finely to continue this progress. Rather, fine splitting is even more critical here, because we are asking the dog to interrupt his own arousal and make a choice, and if the leap is too great compared to what he has done thus far, we're giving him the opportunity to make the wrong choice.

Thus far he has seen only a very still dog, at a distance, facing entirely away. There are many other criteria we might use:

- A jingle of dog tags on a handheld collar (no decoy dog present)
- Decoy dog facing to one side, perpendicular to the learner dog
- Decoy dog facing the learner dog but maintaining eye contact with his handler
- Decoy dog facing the learner dog and making light eye contact (See Chapter 10 for teaching this controlled behavior to the decoy dog, if necessary)
- Decoy dog moving slowly, laterally to learner dog
- Decoy dog trotting laterally
- Decoy dog running laterally
- Decoy dog jumping in air alongside handler
- Decoy dog barking facing away from learner dog
- Decoy dog barking facing learner dog, eyes on handler
- Decoy dog walking slowly toward learner dog
- Decoy dog walking at a diagonal to learner dog
- And any other criteria your learner dog says are difficult for him!

The order presented here is not necessarily the order of difficulty for *your* particular dog; some dogs find movement more threatening, while others are more disconcerted by eye contact. Let your dog and your data tell you what to try next.

Keep It Short. No, Really.

I cannot emphasize enough the importance of very short training sessions. While this superficially appears to be simple work — lie on your mat and get a cookie! — this is in fact very, very challenging for the agitated dog, as he wrestles with his own habits and brain chemistry.

Decision fatigue is real. Plan for it.

I recommend individual training sessions of no more than 90 seconds or so, separated with breaks of equal or considerably longer length, and some dogs may be able to do only a bare handful of such sessions at a time. This is normal! Take breaks, short and long, as needed. Pushing beyond the dog's endurance will only hurt your progress.

I plan these sessions carefully according to what I believe will make the dog successful, and I split criteria according to what I believe he can handle successfully. Consequently, I have very, very rarely seen a dog make the wrong choice and come aggressively off the mat. The few times it did happen, we had trained too long and the dog was beyond his mental endurance.

As I often say to clients, "He's doing great — let's quit before it has a chance to go bad."

Decision fatigue[28] is a real phenomenon[29], and once the dog has reached his limit, he cannot make the choice we want. That failed repetition will be just as memorable to him, or more, as one in which he chose to turn away and relax. Don't risk it.

No Mistakes

Our goal for these sessions is zero errors, or darned close to

> ## Decision Fatigue & Glucose
>
> *Want yet another reason to use food in this training?*
>
> *The brain depletes glucose rapidly during self-control work (such as this) but can recover faster and continue longer with a glucose supplement. Feeding treats can actually help the dogs think better, longer!*

zero errors. It is *my* job as trainer to set up the scenario properly, split criteria finely, and end the session before the dog becomes too fatigued to perform correctly.

As with adding a trigger to the mat, I consider it critical that the dog make all the decisions about his behavior. This means that the humans do no prompting, verbal or physical, outside of providing the mat. If the dog sees the trigger and the handler cues him to go to the mat, did he

---

[28] Decision fatigue refers to the impaired decision-making process as the brain literally becomes tired. A good primer: Tierney, John. "Do You Suffer From Decision Fatigue?" *The New York Times*. [New York City] 17 August 2011. <http://nyti.ms/W4oIJW>

[29] Gailliot, MT, Baumeister, RF, DeWall, CN, Maner, JK, Plant, EA, Tice, DM, Brewer, LE, Schmeichel, BJ. Self-Control Relies on Glucose as a Limited Energy Source: Willpower Is More Than a Metaphor. 2007.

go to the mat because he chose to relax, or because he had an outside prompt? If the latter, what will he do when he does not receive that prompt?

Certainly being able to respond to an outside cue in the presence of the trigger is a good thing! but we are working toward the dog being able to self-assess and interrupt his own arousal. If we don't give him a chance to work entirely on his own, he cannot practice that, and we cannot assess if he is capable of it.

It's difficult for many handlers, especially if nervous about the dog's potential reaction, to be quiet and let him work, speaking only to praise his correct decision. That's okay — we can split criteria for humans, too!

A Sidebar for Science

So, scientifically speaking, what's going on here and why does it work?

This approach utilizes a number of behavioral and psychological phenomena.

> Classical counter-conditioning is occurring as the learner relaxes and receives desirables in the presence of the trigger stimulus.
> Operant counter-conditioning is occurring as the learner consciously chooses an alternate behavior and experiences reinforcement in the presence of the trigger stimulus.
> Systematic desensitization is occurring as the learner

is exposed to managed, successive iterations of the trigger stimulus.

Positive reinforcement appears in the form of tasty food (which also helps physiologically calm the learner) earned by conscious behaviors.

Negative reinforcement is used as the trigger stimulus retreats when the learner chooses an alternate response and relaxes.

By blending all of these approaches, we can see more rapid progress. After several sessions, we should see Dozer making the choice more readily to retreat to his mat and lie comfortably down.

Where Do We Go From Here?

In our hypothetical subject Dozer's case, since we described him as dragging his owners after other dogs in a frenzy, we might simply want him to be calm at the sight of other dogs.

Once Dozer is showing 80% success at each successive level, working with the decoy dog nearer and nearer, we can begin integrating other behaviors along with the mat-work[30]. We might ask him to target and then go to the mat, or sit, or perhaps both. As Dozer builds confidence and reliability, we might ask for some loose-leash walking to the mat. Almost always we'll work toward

---

[30] Leslie McDevitt describes this very well in her book *Control Unleashed*.

105

the mat, ending with mat-work, because it is what Dozer knows and trusts best. By pairing it with other behaviors (always behaviors he has already learned in other contexts first!), we are building confidence in those as well.

Eventually we might phase out the mat-work and simply keep a high rate of reinforcement for the other behaviors, watching our data closely as we progress.

The training plan you develop will depend on your individual situation and goals. Keep in mind that finely split criteria is the key! And watch your data.

Crutches Are Fine

Sometimes a client gives me an update on their progress and then tentatively asks, "Is it okay that I've been carrying the mat with me when we walk? I have a little one that folds into a pocket, but I just feel better being able to pull it out if something happens...."

Yes, it is *more* than okay — it is the sign of a thoughtful trainer! Having a contingency plan is far better than being caught unprepared.

Yes, the mat is a crutch, of course. Yes, using the mat on the walk means the dog still needs aid. But needing aid and having it ready sure beats denying the need for help and losing ground.

Many clients report they are using the matwork at the vet, when traveling to visit friends or family, or other places where their dogs might need some help to settle calmly. I think that's fantastic.

"If your child carried a favorite teddy bear," I ask worried clients, "or a security blanket, and it helped him to feel safe or relax, would you let him take it to the doctor or the dentist? Of course you would! Does that mean he'll also need to take it to college? No. He'll make progress in his own time; you don't need to worry about it."

On the other hand, some clients find the mat so effective and so convenient that they don't see the need to graduate from it; it's easy and helpful at the vet's office, so why try to wean away from it? And that's fine, too. Just remember to also practice without the mat, just in case you're caught one day without it.

Chapter 10 Making the Trigger a Target

THIS IS
CHAUCER.

Rewarding dogs for looking at objects or beings which distract them seems counter-intuitive, but it can be quite effective. Leslie McDevitt helped popularize the procedure in her justly-famous book *Control Unleashed*, describing a training game she dubbed "Look At That" (now often abbreviated as LAT in online discussion).

The technique feels odd and even frightening to some handlers — "but if I treat him for looking at the trigger, he'll focus even more on the trigger!" — but there are other principles of behavior science at play here, and when done properly this is an excellent exercise.

How is it done?

When the dog looks at the trigger, immediately click and then offer a treat[31]. (If the dog is barking or lunging at the trigger, you are too near the trigger or too slow to click.) When the dog eats and looks at the trigger again, click

---

[31] We'll see the best ways to do this in just a moment!

Making the Trigger a Target | Fired Up, Frantic, and Freaked Out

and treat again.

Repeat.

Contrary to what one might think, this does not reinforce fixating on the trigger, but rather reduces the distraction value of the trigger. By making the looking behavior an operant task performed for reward, instead of an emotionally-driven reactive behavior, the behavior around the trigger becomes calmer, more thoughtful and deliberate, and altogether less unpleasant.

This exercise was the first behavior I ever clicked!

I came reluctantly to clicker training with a reactive dog whose behavior was getting progressively worse with the compulsive methods I knew. All I knew of clicker training was that I was supposed to click for what I wanted — and it seemed to me that I wanted Chaucer to look at other dogs without barking. So I clicked immediately as she looked at another dog, before she could bark, and gave her a treat.

Chaucer caught on right away, and I was sold on clicker training. I didn't have a clue yet about why my experiment had worked -- but I knew it worked!

Decoy Dog

This is also a very valuable exercise for a decoy dog to know, as it allows the introduction of controlled eye contact in a very unemotional way for the learner dog. The eye contact is brief and relatively unthreatening, because the decoy dog really isn't even interested in the learner dog.

There's little risk of the decoy dog actually engaging with

the learner dog, as he's just using the learner dog to earn his treats.

Make It Better

This exercise again works on several behavioral fronts, which is what makes it so effective.

- Classical counter-conditioning is utilized when the dog associates the sight of the trigger with the click and treat.
- Operant conditioning is utilized when the dog deliberately chooses to look at the trigger (instead of reactively or emotionally looking at the trigger).
- Desensitization is utilized when the dog looks away (to get the treat) before reaching threshold.
- Positive reinforcement is used in the form of tasty food (which also helps physiologically calm the learner).

There's a reason this exercise is popular! But we should be sure to cover a few points which are often overlooked....

Treat Away

In order to get the benefit of desensitization, we must manage the trigger's exposure. Unless we are somehow influencing the dog's gaze, we aren't taking advantage of that.

Pulling the dog away or blocking his view, while recommended by some, have drawbacks and fallout

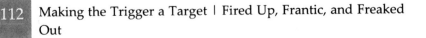

we'd prefer to avoid. It's simplicity itself, however, to simply offer the earned treat on the other side of the dog's head, inducing him to turn away from the sight of the trigger.

In addition, this type of delivery gives us all kinds of information about the dog's state of mind!

- 🐾 Does he turn immediately upon hearing the click and immediately takes the treat, as gently as he has been taught? The dog is calm and focused.
- 🐾 Does he delay for a second or so after the click and before turning for this treat? The dog is stressed, either distracted from the marker or afraid to take his eyes from the trigger; in either case, he's not going to learn efficiently.
- 🐾 Does the dog turn readily but take the treats more sharply than usual? This dog is stressed as well.
- 🐾 Is he failing to turn away to retrieve his treat? This dog is on the point of losing it — bail out!

Treat Discretely

Deliver each treat for a single, discrete, marked behavior. If we feed continuously while the dog continues to look at the trigger, we are losing the opportunity and advantage of a reset and distinct, discrete repetitions.

Discrete repetitions not only make for far easier success rate data collection — and you are still keeping data, right? — but they make for simpler assessment of a dog's current stress level, as mentioned above. I also firmly believe that discrete repetitions keep that stress level lower by providing many micro-breaks within the training session itself.

In short, feeding the dog while he looks at the trigger, with or without a clicker, is simply classical counter-conditioning alone. There's a great deal to be said for classical counter-conditioning, of course, but it's not the same as a more operant game, and why limit ourselves?

"Pavlov is always on your shoulder"

This catchphrase from Bob Bailey reminds us that classical conditioning is inherent in everything we do — even operant conditioning[32].

Many trainers and handlers spend time in classically counter-conditioning dogs to the sight or sound of triggers, and certainly there's nothing wrong with this.

The trouble with classical conditioning, however, is that is often takes a long time. While associations of fear or pain can be made in very few repetitions, even to single-event learning experiences (how many times will the proverbial cat jump onto the hot stove burner again?), more pleasant associations typically take several or many repetitions, and far more if they need to recover ground

---

[32] There is also research to indicate that operant conditioning is inherent in everything we do, even classical conditioning — but that's material for another time!

from unpleasant ones. It's not uncommon for training plans relying primarily on classical counter-conditioning to require weeks or months of consistent work.

I'm often asked why I use a clicker, which seems like more effort and complication. I reply, "Because I'm lazy."

Why? To speak in the terms of our limbic/rational continuum, classical conditioning — also called respondent conditioning — relies solely on the reactive side of our continuum. The dog doesn't have to think, isn't asked to think, and probably won't actually think. There's nothing rational about it, only reactive — and the dog's already practiced at reactive, usually not in the way we want (which is why we have a training problem in the first place).

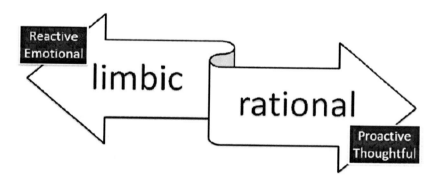

By kicking over to the rational end of the mental continuum, we're engaging the brain in a new way, a way it hasn't looked at the trigger before — and we can make much faster progress. Unlike respondent conditioning, which typically requires multiple repetitions, operant conditioning takes effect as soon as the dog recognizes the game, and one-trial learning is fairly common among clicker-trained animals.

And because Pavlov is always on our shoulder, we're still getting all the benefits of classical conditioning, as well. Two for the price of one!

Chapter 11 Why It Goes Wrong

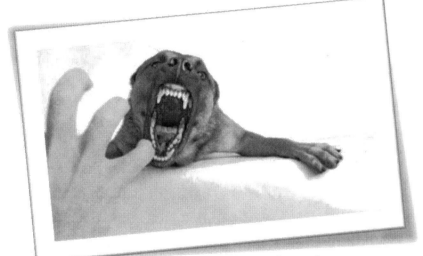

DON'T TRY THIS
AT HOME!

There are two very common reasons for failure.

Progressing Too Quickly

It is unfortunately easy to raise criteria more rapidly than the dog can handle. Yes, this training often moves far more quickly than expected — but let's not get greedy.

Leaping ahead may not immediately show poor results, but you're laying a thin foundation rather than a strong one, and under stress the behavior will likely buckle. Then, at a more advanced level, the dog appears inexplicably stubborn or confused, incapable of meeting standard. A quick look at the data will show, however, a lack of solid 80% or better success rates leading up to this — or even no data at all! -- and consequently the dog has little to build on.

This too-rapid progression can take several forms.

Skips in Criteria

This is probably the most common error; after all, *we*

know the end goal, so skipping ahead often seems logical to us. It's easy to assume the dog knows where we're going as well.

> *A student came to me after a holiday break. "That mat thing doesn't work," she said.*
>
> *I was surprised. "But he was doing so well in his first session, lying right down as soon as he saw the mat. What's not working now?"*
>
> *"Well, I wanted to use the mat for keeping him quiet at the door, like you said we could. I had 17 people coming for Thanksgiving dinner, so that seemed like a good time to have him quiet. But he got right off the mat and ran around with the other dog, tripping people and sniffing at all the food. It was crazy, and the mat didn't help at all."*

It shouldn't be too difficult to see the trouble here — the dog's first matwork session had been alone and with minimal distraction, while his second had been with another excited dog and 17 strangers carrying tempting food!

That's an extreme example of leaping ahead in criteria, but leaps happen all the time. Remember, our goal is to make our many steps so incremental and smooth that the progression feels almost seamless.

Keep in mind my unscientific-but-useful rule of thumb: a single mistake is a mistake or a question; the same mistake twice in a row indicates that the dog did not recognize or absorb feedback from the first mistake. That's a good sign that you're moving too quickly.

Leaving the Plan

I also see handlers move ahead in the training plan not by accident, but knowingly, assuming that since the dog had been doing so well, they can move more quickly.

Unfortunately, I see this error most often in clients with fear-aggressive dogs. I think they want to see improvement so badly — they want their dogs to be comfortable and their social risk reduced — that they convince themselves they can jump ahead.

What this handler doesn't realize, as they decide to leave the training plan, is that the dog was doing so well precisely because of that training plan. The structure was there to build the dog's new skills and his own confidence in those skills. Moving too quickly, even though the dog appears to be doing well, undermines that reliability and confidence, making a setback more likely.

And it is always more difficult and time-consuming to recover from a setback than to baby-step all the way.

If the dog seems to be beating the training plan and is looking happy and confident, *great!* Keep up the good work! And remember how you got this far — with incremental steps and a high rate of reinforcement.

Sessions Too Long

This is an unfortunately easy step to make. We get caught up in the dog's success and lose track of the time, or we simply don't want to invest time in setting up and preparing to train for only a minute or so of work.

"The one to stop is the one before you say 'just one more,'" said wise trainer Steve White, and it is even more true when dealing with conflicted or emotional learners. Clicker training sessions are generally short anyway, but when working in this vein I usually recommend sessions of just 30-90 seconds.

As mentioned before, the dog's task may look outwardly simple — lie on a comfy mat and eat treats! — but the task of staying rational and focused when habit and sometimes fear draws him toward an emotional reaction can actually be quite tiring. Short sessions not only prevent errors, by quitting before decision fatigue makes it more difficult to make the right choices, but keep training from feeling like a chore to the dog. If many training sessions end with an exhausted dog, he won't look forward to them, and we definitely want him regarding this as a game rather than another stressful event!

Don't worry if your dog seems to need incredibly short sessions to be happy and successful. His endurance will grow as he becomes more comfortable and confident with the process and his new skills.

> *I had one client bring an anxious dog for training, and he was so worried about things that he could not do more than a single target or two before he would make mistakes or simply quit.*
>
> *I instructed her to do just a single rep per session. It felt dreadfully slow to an owner who had trained other, more receptive dogs before, but she did it — and less than a year later, certified him as a therapy dog in a field they both enjoyed.*

Make the task as easy as it needs to be in order to get started successfully. You can always make it harder as you get better.

Chapter 12 Medication and the Agitated Dog

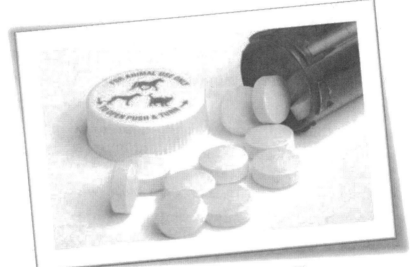

Is this an option?

When, if ever, are drugs appropriate?

Any discussion here must necessarily be superficial, as my state law prevents any non-veterinarian from discussing prescription drugs professionally. But I do recognize client dogs in need of medical treatment as well as behavioral, and I refer these to a qualified veterinarian for diagnosis and perhaps a prescription.

Any time medication arises in discussion with training, some common myths and assumptions surface as well. Let's look at these.

My dog needs drugs.

Probably not. Most ill-mannered dogs I meet are simply that, dogs who have not yet learned better manners. Even most annoyingly hyper dogs and most frightened dogs are simply expressing behaviorally what they have learned, and drugs won't change that.

My dog doesn't need drugs.

Maybe. But if a qualified professional (such as your trainer) recommends that you ask a qualified veterinarian about possible treatment, it's not because we get a kickback from the vet or the drug company. (We don't.)

After many, many dogs, I have a pretty good idea of the average progression through this type of work. When a dog doesn't stay on course, either the training needs adjusted or the dog does. Quite often it's the training; training records show the dog hasn't had enough sessions, or criteria jumps were too large, or the dog needs a different presentation of trigger stimuli (aural instead of visual, etc.).

Sometimes, though, a professional can see that the training just isn't "taking" in the dog's mind. And this is always, without exception, in dogs which exhibit anxiety.

Just as in humans, dogs who are worried don't learn well. And if the brain, through genetics or conditioning, is in a state of chronic worry, it's not going to absorb training.

I have worked with dogs who would start to relax on their mats and then jerk into a tense state again, because lying comfortably was so foreign to them it felt untenable. Can you imagine what that must be like? In his own kitchen, surrounded by his own family, and he's unable to relax even for pay? This is heart-breaking, and one of the reasons I believe failing to treat an anxious dog is actually cruel.

These dogs need medication (usually temporary) to allow the training to take hold.

Drugs will fix my dog.

Appropriate medication will allow the brain to recognize and process the information training provides; it does not teach the dog new skills or coping mechanisms on its own. For permanent change, training is necessary.

What do you mean, my dog is anxious? My dog's not anxious.

Many owners just don't see the problem.

> *I'd been called for housetraining issues and barking, but a few minutes in the house were enough to show me these were just symptoms of a greater concern.*
>
> *I pointed out the dog's ear position, the body posture, the angle of the tail, the eye movements, the lip licks, the yawns. I explained that these were all signs of stress and that the dog was anxious.*
>
> *"Nah, I don't think so," said the owners. "She looks like that all the time."*

Because canine anxiety can look different from human anxiety, because its symptoms are often confused with bad manners[33] or misguided concepts of social hierarchy[34], and because many portrayals of dogs in pop culture actually depict stressed behaviors as normal[35] or even desirable[36], many owners don't recognize anxiety as the root of their dogs' troubles[37].

This isn't the space to explore why anxiety appears so often in pet dogs (though I will briefly mention that genetics and poor socialization are two very common culprits), but the fact is, it does, and it's only humane and efficient to treat it.

Drugs will "dope up" my dog.

Not if prescribed and used properly! This is a common myth which sadly prevents many owners from getting help for their anxious dogs. But the right drug, in the

---

[33] Barking, jumping up, and soiling the house all are common behavior problems which can be rooted in either simple lack of training or anxiety.

[34] No, peeing in the house is not a sign that a dog is bidding to move up the social ladder, any more than wetting the bed is a sign that a human toddler is a future megalomaniac. Why do these myths persist? See the Appendix for more information on dominance and its misunderstanding.

[35] It's startling, once one recognizes stress in dogs, how many dogs in advertising photos, etc. are displaying these key signs and are presented as normal or cute.

[36] Some trainers promote signs of distress as signs of respectful submission — untrue and perhaps even cruel.

[37] The Appendix includes a list of behaviors which can indicate stress in a dog; it's a good idea to compare your dog's behavior against that to see if she might in fact be in distress.

right dose, will *not* affect your dog in this way.

I tell owners who are hesitant to try medication that they shouldn't see any change in their dog's personality — it will be the same dog, just less anxious. It's having all the things you like about your dog, undiluted.

Any vet can prescribe for my dog.

Maybe. Or, yes, this is technically true, but it's good to ask questions, anyway.

I have the greatest respect for veterinarians, who face an enormous job. In a typical morning a vet might treat a dog for diabetes, perform emergency surgery on a cat hit by a car, and diagnose cancer in a lizard. While human doctors frequently have the luxury of specialization or referrals to specialists, most veterinarians have to keep up not only with many fields of medicine, but across many species!

I don't think it is disrespectful then to say that it is unfair to expect them to keep up with behavior as well. That's not their job.

Legally, any licensed veterinarian can prescribe pyscho-pharmaceuticals for a client. However, most veterinarians aren't necessarily fluent in the latest behavior options and treatments. For this reason, I refer my training clients, if necessary, to a vet who also specializes in behavior. (I have several names on file, to allow for geographic location or personal preference.)

Why does this matter? Because the wrong prescription can not only be useless, which is frustrating and demoralizing to the owner, but can actually make things worse, which can be dangerous.

Case #1

A woman told me her dog was afraid of storms, and they were using the prescribed acepromazine to control it. Even after eight years of "treatment," the dog's storm phobia had gotten progressively worse, and if they didn't get the dose into the dog in time, the dog's terror was extreme.

Some vets still use tranquilizers for anxiety or phobias, but this is decidedly not recommended. Ace is a dopamine antagonist and an anti-psychotic drug; giving it to dogs who are not psychotic (i.e., not schizophrenic, etc.) results in a loss of motor control[38].

This appears to work well as a tranquilizer, but it makes the root problem worse. The animal is still just as afraid — but now is unable to act on his fears. Have you ever had that nightmare where you know something terrible is coming and you just can't move?

It's not hard to see, once we think about it, that the inability to control one's body are not likely to make a

---

[38] Sternberg, Lynn Kerlin Paul. Email interview. 2012, November 19.

frightened animal less upset about the situation — rather the opposite! And the problem is likely to worsen as a result.

It is thought also that acepromazine, often prescribed for noise phobias, actually *increases* sensitivity to noise[39], but that the animal simply cannot express its fear or reactions.

Using acepromazine or a similar drug directly inhibits learning and prolongs the problem.

And it's important to remember that dopamine is crucial to operant learning, and using a dopamine antagonist drug directly interferes with any training to teach the dog better coping skills or alternate behaviors.

Ace and similar drugs may win the battle of keeping a dog conveniently sedated for a single event, but they certainly lose the war in long-term training and associations. For these reasons, their use has generally fallen out of favor in the treatment of anxiety by veterinary behaviorists.

Case #2
A client told me she disliked the idea of drugs for her

---

[39] Overall, KL. "Storm Phobias." *DVM Newsmagazine* September 2004: 13-15.

dog because she hadn't liked the effect on a previous dog. "He would stagger and walk right into walls," she described. "He couldn't respond to anything. It worked, he wasn't afraid, but it was terrible. The vet said it wasn't a problem, but I hated it."

I reassured her that this was *not* typical — in fact, I had used the same event drug for a storm-phobic dog myself, and there was no discernible difference except that she could stay calm and work on her relaxation protocol during the storm. Drug choice and dosage do matter!

Case #3

I had a client whose young dog was exhibiting signs of anxiety. I had been seeing them for basic manners and was able to advise them of the tendencies, recommending they take steps before the behaviors grew worse. I recommended a vet visit, with a behavior-savvy vet, to ask about possible medication.

The client's own vet said there was no reason to go to another clinic, he could prescribe drugs for them, and he did. When the client updated me, I recognized that the drug he'd chosen was a popular behavior drug but usually used in other scenarios, and I encouraged her to call the behavior vet. She said there was no need.

About a week later, she called back; the dog had bitten her child in an unprecedented incident. The popular drug, very useful in other situations, had simply lowered her anxious dog's inhibitions here, and now instead of an anxious dog, she had both an anxious child and an anxious dog with a bite history.

It is worth asking one's vet if he or she is well-versed in current behavior treatment, and it is no shame to them if they concentrate their continuing education in other area. (It's actually a great sign that they're aware of their limits!) Behavior is a specialty like any other; find the right partner to help you and your dog.

Chapter 13 Preventative Measures

HOW COULD THESE
CUTE FACES GROW UP
TO BE A PROBLEM?

If the best cure is prevention, how can a thoughtful owner take steps to avoid needing this book?

I mentioned in Chapter 4 that both genetics and environment influence a dog's behavior, reactivity threshold, and outlook on the world in general. An owner has choices in both of these, and some thought and planning early on can save a lifetime of stress, effort, and frustration.

Socialization

Socialization is *vital* for proper mental and social development. In fact, I think it's probable most trainers would say the lack of socialization is the single biggest cause of problems in their clientele. The dog who growls at strangers, the dog who gets frantic and greets visitors too roughly, the dog who nips at kids, the dog who needs muzzled at the vet, the dog who goes ballistic at the sight of another dog on walks — all of these are often rooted in a lack of proper socialization.

Most people have heard by now that socialization is

important. The stumbling block is that many people still don't know what good socialization looks like.

I blogged a series called "When You Should NOT Socialize Your Dog," on common "socialization" practices which I observed created more problems than they prevented. It prompted discussion among trainers who had seen many of the same problems in their own clientele. So let's look at what good socialization should be.

What Does Socialization Do?

I am not terribly fond of the term "socialization," which despite its technical definition is I think too easy for new puppy owners to interpret simply as, "Meet people." I would like to suggest a new definition that all new dog owners embrace fully — *socialization is introduction to various entities and stimuli for the purposes of teaching how to meet challenges and cope with stress.*

"I don't know why he's like this! He's never had any bad experiences with that."

"How many good experiences has he had?"

A good socialization session introduces a puppy or dog to something new, maybe even challenges them a little, and leaves them with a good experience. *Yep, that was a weird floor surface, but we learned how to play on it and we had a really cool game. Yep, that guy had the weirdest hat ever, but he knew how to do the target game for treats!*

How Not To Do It

The problem is, as mentioned above, not with socialization but with many people's understanding of the word and their assumptions. Remember that socialization is showing a puppy new things and letting the puppy "win" in whatever challenge was presented. Too often, though, people think only of showing the puppy new things. If the puppy does not leave the challenge feeling more confident and happy than when he met it, he did not have a good socialization experience. Thus, sometimes what they intend as socialization in fact creates far more problems than it prevents.

This is easy to do with puppies, or with dogs who show stress by growing quiet instead of loud[40].

> *One owner explained to me how he had taken care to socialize his young puppy to kids. Every few days he had taken the puppy to the nearby elementary school, letting dozens of children gather around the pup and pet and hold and shout excitedly and run around it. "She never minded," he said. "She liked it. She just sat*

---

[40] There are two main categories of stress reaction. Dogs who stress "down" slow their movements, go still, and are often mistaken for "good dogs" or calm dogs, though internally they are anything but calm. Dogs who stress "up" get frantic and vocal, and they draw far more attention to themselves. These dogs are much more annoying, but they often get help first!

still while they rubbed her all over and everything."

He called for help after the adult dog bit a toddler.

What had seemed a perfect socialization opportunity to this well-meaning owner had in fact been a nightmare for his puppy, overwhelmed and without any means of retreat. Because she was quiet and still, and probably even exhibited some tail-wagging and licking and other please-I'm-just-a-puppy-don't-hurt-me appeasement behaviors, it may have looked like the pup was learning to like kids. As she grew older, however, she ceased the puppy appeasement behaviors and concluded that the best defense is a good offense.

If the puppy does not leave the challenge feeling more confident and happy than when he met it, he did not have a good socialization experience.

Several dozen children at once is an extreme example, but I actually see variations on this scenario too often. Any time the puppy is not actively enjoying the socialization experience, at least by the end — it's okay if he learns to overcome a short challenge — you're potentially doing more harm than good.

Socialize the Right Way

To avoid future trouble, check this socialization guidelines list:

* Does the puppy have an escape route? (Can he move away from the motorcycle or the funny hat or the other dog? Be sure that he can — and that he knows it's available[41].)
* Is he using the escape route repeatedly, or is he reluctant to come back to the challenge? (If so, the challenge is probably too challenging at this point.)
* Is he coming back to the challenge of his own volition? (That's a good thing, keeping the challenge at a level with his curiosity!)
* Are you using food to lure him back?

This last, using food to encourage a puppy into a socialization situation is very common, but in my opinion it's a mistake.

A puppy following food does not indicate a comfortable puppy, only attractive food. It's even possible for a puppy feeling a bit overwhelmed to focus on the food as a sort of escape mechanism: "I'm looking at this fascinating food, not the scary thing!"

I sometimes see puppies drawn into an uncomfortable location by food, and then when the food is gone they look up and "suddenly" have a fear reaction. In fact the fear is not new; we were just concealing it.

---

[41] Never assume a dog knows an escape route is available to him. Sometimes they don't see it, or often adult dogs have not been allowed to leave a scary situation previously and don't realize that we'll let them take advantage of it.

I often warn clients of what I call the "candy from strangers" phenomenon — a lure into a potentially scary situation signifies a scary situation. If the puppy has to be lured into interaction, something's wrong!

If the puppy approaches or targets a scary object or person, and then is reinforced with food, that's different — that's a contract fulfilled, and it builds the puppy's confidence in the system. "Even if it's scary, my cues still work out for my own good!"

Kathy Sdao, an associate certified applied animal behaviorist, puts it in different terms when she warns of the danger of "poisoning the food" just as we must be careful of poisoning cues. It's not too difficult to teach dogs that the presentation of food means something scary, painful, or otherwise aversive is about to happen — and then you've lost the ability to use a very powerful reinforcer to help train the dog through that fear.

We use lots of food in training, of course — but food is for rewarding, not bribing!

Socialization Later in Life

Sometimes owners acquire dogs later in life, or realize too late that they missed puppy socialization, and they attempt to "make up" time by taking the dogs out to socialize.

This isn't necessarily a bad idea — better late than never!

While defined socialization periods are key and owners shouldn't miss them if they can possibly help it, there can be benefit to other exposure. But there are several points to keep in mind during this:

- 🐾 An over-excited, ill-mannered dog isn't learning socialization skills; he's practicing being over-excited and ill-mannered.
- 🐾 An over-whelmed dog isn't learning socialization skills; he's confirming that the world is indeed a scary place.
- 🐾 An older dog has no "puppy license"[42] and likely to find less tolerance (with both dogs and humans) if it has hesitations or ill manners.

Even if your over-excited dog is basically friendly, putting him in a scenario where other dogs are likely to be angry at him isn't going to help him socialize.

This is equally true for "friendly" aroused dogs ("he just wants to say hi!") and "aggressive" aroused dogs. Picture an overeager friendly dog, pulling hard, panting or gasping, eyes intent on the new dog it wants to befriend — and on the receiving end, it can look very aggressive or very predatory, and it often prompts a very defensive reaction.

Even if your over-excited dog is basically friendly,

---

[42] This is the phenomenon which enables us to more easily forgive young and cute things when they err.

putting him in a scenario where other dogs are likely to be angry at him isn't going to help him socialize.

> *I met a dog once at an entertainment event. The owners had just acquired the young adult dog and wanted to socialize it, since it had never been out of its first environment, so they brought it with them to an hours-long event of several hundred people. The dog was absolutely petrified and, far from being socialized, was learning that, Yep, the world is indeed terrifying!*
>
> *"But she isn't barking," they observed, so they assumed it was working. Nope, she was just a dog who stressed down[43] instead of up, and the problem was only getting worse. (They chose to bring her again the next time, so she would learn. It was heartbreaking.)*

If you take an older dog out to socialize, plan your outing carefully and stay aware of your dog. If you are not willing to bail out if your dog needs it, do not take the dog with you. And if your dog is too aroused or stressed and cannot recover, you need to quit before you create more problems.

People attending a community event did not sign up to rehabilitate a troubled dog; they came to enjoy a social outing. Putting a stressed dog in their midst neither helps the dog nor enhances their enjoyment. At best it only confirms public opinion that dogs are often nuisances and should be banned from public areas or events; at worst, it creates more problems for the dog and puts

---

[43] (see footnote 40)

people or other dogs in danger.

Instead, match the outing to the dog's current skill set. Has this dog ever been on a field trip to a group event? If not, then starting at the street fair with new asphalt substrates, a thousand people, several dozen food vendors, other (possibly stressed) dogs, and the roar of engines from the car show is probably not a good choice for an outing. How about starting with the neighbor's cookout, where you can introduce him to fewer people and then pop him back home after he's had a good time?

The aforementioned guidelines for good socialization (escape route, appropriate challenge, happy ending) all apply to socializing the older dog as well.

Genetics

This can be a touchy subject, but that's no reason to ignore it. Yes, nurture matters — but so does nature.

> *A man brought a dog for training. The dog, approximately a year old, was one of the more dangerous individuals with which we've worked, very serious in his aggression and very slow to change his behavior.*
>
> *"He's always been like this," the owner explained. "Not exactly like this, of course, but he was growling and snapping when I went to see his litter when they were seven weeks old."*
>
> *We asked, as diplomatically as possible, why he would even consider bringing home such an obviously*

> *troubled puppy to his children.*
>
> *"I figured I could handle it, and he would change. Puppies are just what you make them."*

Many times I think people shy away from discussing genetic influences on temperament because they fear it will lend credibility to travesties such as breed-specific legislation[44], and they don't want to support such ridiculous actions.

But while it is very true that a dog's breed does not determine his behavior, it is also true that a dog's individual parentage can play a role. Remember our limbic/rational continuum.

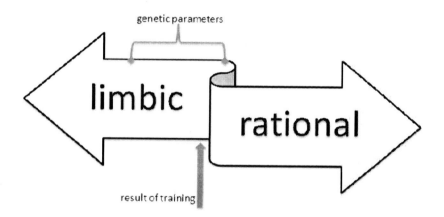

In this model, training and environment set the dog's actual position within the parameters set by his genetics.

---

[44] BSL is the banning of certain breeds or physical types of dog in the belief that it is breed which makes a dog dangerous, and that banning such breeds will prevent dog bites. It doesn't, and it doesn't.

This is particularly true with anxiety and fearfulness; it is well-documented that genetic shyness and anxiety travel in familial lines[45].

I have sometimes been asked to help a fearful dog where it has come up in conversation that the dog's sire, or dam, or elder sibling was the same way. Why was a dog with such a temperament permitted to breed? And equally valid, why would anyone purposefully choose a puppy from a bloodline with faulty temperament?[46]

It should be noted that I am certainly *not* saying all fearful dogs come from fearful parents, nor that genetically-influenced anxiety cannot appear from what seem to be "normal" parents. Breeding, even at the best of times, is a calculated gamble.

But we can, and should, gamble with those odds in our favor. While there's a small chance that a reactive dog could come out of a normal background, there's an equally-small chance that a normal dog will come out of a reactive background.

---

[45] Overall KL, Dunham AE. A protocol for predicting performance in military working dogs: roles for anxiety assessment and genetic markers. 2005.

[46] And as long as I'm on my soapbox, "But I didn't know what the parents were like" is a protest which answers itself.

This is so much irrelevant babble, however, to those who inherited a dog, adopted one from a shelter, took a stray off the street, etc. And we certainly don't expect — or want! — those owners to give up and start over with new dogs.

However or wherever we acquired our new family member, he's family now, and as we've seen, there's a lot that can be done with an "imperfect" dog.

If we look at our continuum again, we can see that a well-trained dog with a genetic proclivity toward reactive behavior may in fact be more thoughtful and rational than a neglected dog with a less-reactive predisposition.

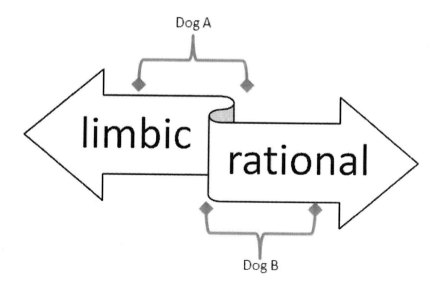

I am often asked by clients, "But *why* is he this way?"

"I can't say for certain," I answer. "I can make an educated guess, of course, but I can't put the dog on the couch and ask if he hated his father. Odds are he never ever knew his father, anyway. And even if we did know why he's this way, we'd still have to train him — so let's save time and just start with that."

Merely lamenting the dog's past changes nothing. No matter what the background or how we came here, we work with the dog we have.

Consider Medication As Necessary

If the dog we have is challenged with a less-helpful set of genetics, and he is struggling, it is only fair to consider medical intervention. Physical problems may need physical solutions, and if we are working with a dog which just doesn't have enough dopamine in his system, it's perhaps even unethical to deny a cure.

Genetic anxiety is associated with slower learning — meaning, the dog who most needs to adopt new coping skills is also the dog who will have the greatest difficulty doing so. Help him if he needs it. See Chapter 12 for more discussion on medication and anxious or fearful behavior.

Chapter 14 In The End

SHAKESPEARE DEMONSTRATES
"CHILL ON A MAT"

I had been invited to give a training demonstration at the Indiana State Museum, for a new (now annual) event celebrating pets. It's a great museum, and I was pleased to have been asked.

The parking garage opens directly into the museum, so Laevatein and I couldn't see anything of the day's visitors or layout before we went inside. I slipped the loop of her leash over my wrist and, arms loaded with crate, props, and gear, headed inside.

The central atrium of the museum is a gorgeous multistory affair, opening onto the old canal and containing a full façade rescued from a historic building. It echoes on the best of days, and it was far louder than usual on this particular day, as I realized the event had not been completely explained to me.

What you must understand is that Laevatein is a very low-threshold dog; she is easily stimulated by things which would not bother most other dogs. She is hyperpredatory, having been described by those with decades of experience in working and protection sport dogs as off-the-chart for even that specialized population.

So when I saw that not only was the city shelter present with about thirty barking, jumping dogs and mewling cats, but the local ferret club had brought a dozen ferrets and the herpetology association had perhaps two dozen lizards and snakes sitting on display, with some being carried through the crowd — well, I had a moment of shock and pure terror.

At the end of the leash, Laev went rigid. Her hackles were raised all down her back, and her tail was so high it arched over her spine. I wasn't sure she was even breathing, as she tried to process this scene which managed to be simultaneously a threatening sea of chaos and a target-rich environment. My arms were full of gear; while I had her leash over my arm, I knew I couldn't react fast enough to prevent the imminent nuclear meltdown.

And then Laev simply folded her legs and dropped into a down, without any cue from me. She took a couple of breaths, visibly relaxed, and then stood again and looked at me with a wag of her tail, as if to say, "Okay, I'm better now. Let's go."

I had been doing a great deal of matwork recently with her, and she had practiced and honed the skill of consciously checking her initial reaction and choosing to relax instead. And she had, in a new and overwhelming environment to which I never would have subjected her so abruptly and without aid, made the unprompted choice to use that skill to remain calm.

I could not have been more proud of her.

Appendix

Stress Indicators

The following are general lists of behaviors which can be used to identify stress in dogs. (Want to learn more about this? See *Canine Behavior: An Illustrated Handbook* by Barbara Handelman, or *The Language of Dogs*, a DVD by Sarah Kalnajs.)

Obviously these behaviors must be observed in context, with an eye to the big picture; a dog licking his lips after eating a peanut butter treat or panting after running on a summer day probably isn't doing so out of stress, while a dog panting in a cool room or licking lips as a child approaches needs attention and intervention.

Behaviors indicating inhibiting stress ("stressing down")

- Becoming quiet or still
- Trembling
- Hiding
- Ears flattened or back
- Tail lowered
- Avoiding eye contact
- Whites of eyes visible
- Sniffing the ground
- Turning head or body away

Behaviors indicating frantic stress ("stressing up")

- High tail
- Very fast tail wags
- Running
- Jumping (on people or objects)
- Barking
- Obnoxious forced interaction
- Pacing

General stress indicators

- Elevated heart rate
- Shedding
- Scratching
- Wet-dog shake
- Lip licks
- Unfocused eyes
- Reluctance to take food
- Reluctance to play
- Yawns
- Panting

Resouces

Socialization

- Dr. Sophia Yin's puppy socialization checklist: http://bit.ly/TI7W5s
- ASVAB position statement on puppy socialization: http://bit.ly/UGUiRn

Dominance & Training

- Dr. Sophia Yin's chapter on The Dominance Controversy, with videos and additional

downloadable content: http://bit.ly/TxercG
- American Veterinary Society of Animal Behavior (ASVAB) position statement on dominance theory in behavior modification: http://bit.ly/VBLlqb
- ASVAB position statement on the use of punishment in behavior modification: http://bit.ly/TxePaW
- *Plenty in Life is Free*, by Kathy Sdao

Finding Professional Help

- ASVAB statement on choosing a trainer: http://bit.ly/VvnsRy
- ASVAB search to find a behavior specialist locally: http://bit.ly/RtFGoI
- The Purdue University Animal Behavior Clinic is an excellent facility with a distance consultation program if you want a referral or are unable to find a behavior-specialist veterinarian locally: http://bit.ly/Vjw6CS

There are many wonderful trainers out there, but also some less helpful; there is no licensing body to separate the educated and skilled from the rest. Look for a certified trainer using the guidelines above. I can also recommend any trainer found at http://bit.ly/TzSx8u, as certified trainers from the Karen Pryor Academy (of which I am a graduate and now faculty) must graduate their courses with an A or not at all. There are of course many excellent trainers with other credentials as well!

Clicker Training Resources

- 🐾 www.ClickerTraining.com
- 🐾 *Click for Joy*, by Melissa Alexander
- 🐾 *Control Unleashed*, by Leslie McDevitt
- 🐾 Your Dog's Personal Trainer video library: http://bit.ly/Ul9UqP
- 🐾 Cyber Dog online training course: http://bit.ly/RtIySi
- 🐾 *Agility Right from the Start*, by Eva Bertilsson and Emelie Johnson Vegh
- 🐾 *The Power of Positive Dog Training*, by Pat Miller
- 🐾 *Puppy Start Right*, by Kenneth Martin and Debbie Martin
- 🐾 *Clicking with Your Dog*, by Peggy Tillman
- 🐾 *The How of Bow-Wow*, DVD by Virginia Broitman and Sherri Lippman

Simple Record Sheet

Criteria	Notes	# Reps	# Correct	Success Rate

Download as printable PDF from www.CaninesInAction.com

Glossary

Arousal — the emotions of excitement, agitation, fear, anger, stress, joy; may be enjoyable or distressing, depending on cause and context.

Classical conditioning — like Pavlov's bell predicting food and causing the dogs to drool, one stimulus is associated with another.

Classical counter-conditioning — pairing a desirable stimulus (special treats) with an undesirable (spiders) to reduce the unpalatability of the undesirable stimulus.

Desensitization — exposure to the stimulus until it ceases to be novel or stimulating; a city dweller ignores traffic noise that might bother a rural visitor.

Latency — the amount of time between a learner perceiving the cue and beginning the appropriate response. This is one aspect of fluency.

Learned irrelevance — the ignoring of unassociated stimuli, or signals which do not convey a significant meaning; often seen when a cue is used too early, before the dog fully understands the associated behavior

Negative reinforcement — subtracting ("negative")

something to make a behavior stronger; fastening a seatbelt ends the annoying car buzzer and thus reinforces seatbelt behavior.

No-Reward Marker — an indicator that a response was incorrect and will not produce reinforcement; think of a wrong-answer buzzer on a game show.

Operant conditioning — the science of consequences affecting behavior. Reinforced behaviors become stronger and occur more frequently; punished or extinguished behaviors become weaker and occur less often.

Positive reinforcement — adding ("positive") something to make a behavior stronger; giving a treat for a sit reinforces sitting behavior.

Reinforcer — any consequence which causes the antecedent behavior to become stronger.

Threshold — the point at which a stimulus becomes "too much" for the subject, whether inducing fear, excitement, etc.

About the Author

Laura VanArendonk Baugh CPDT-KA KPACTP has been working with dogs and horses since childhood, and she began training professionally in 1999. Laura was one of the earliest dog trainers to achieve national certification, scoring 98% on her written exam. She enjoys pursuing continuing education

more than anyone should, and she has presented internationally on behavior.

Laura is particularly fascinated by the science of altering behavior. Her instructional videos are popularly recommended and used in presentations on clicker training, and one has even made its way into a Harvard behavior class!

In January 2008 Laura became a Certified Training Partner with the highly-regarded Karen Pryor Academy for Animal Training & Behavior, and she returned to the Academy as an instructor, teaching certification workshops around the country.

You can find Laura blogging at www.CaninesInAction.com and at www.LauraVanArendonkBaugh.com. She tweets at @CIA_k9s and @Laura_VAB, too!

Index

CPSIA information can be obtained
at www.ICGtesting.com
Printed in the USA
LVOW10s0841120617

537802LV00020B/620/P